WILE E. COYOTE'S

PHYSICAL SCIENCE

FOR SUPER GENIUSES IN TRAINING

written by
Mark Weakland
Suzanne Slade

illustrated by
Christian Cornia
Andrés Martínez Ricci
Loic Billiau
Alan Brown
Paco Sordo

CAPSTONE PRESS
a capstone imprint

Published by Capstone Press,
an imprint of Capstone.
1710 Roe Crest Drive
North Mankato, Minnesota 56003
capstonepub.com

Library of Congress Cataloging-in-Publication Data
is available on the Library of Congress website

ISBN: 9781669032755 (paperback)
ISBN: 9781669032762 (ebook PDF)

Summary: Explores basic physical science concepts, such as
forces and motion, magnetism, states of matter, and more, by
following Wile E. Coyote's wacky attempts to catch Road Runner.

Printed and bound China.   4984

Table of Contents

MEEP! MEEP!

Wile E. Coyote is one clever predator. He thinks he's a super genius. He has invented hundreds of ways to catch Road Runner. But his inventions always tend to fail in unexpected ways. Could it be he still has a lot to learn?

Join Wile E. on his wild and wacky misadventures. This super genius in training will teach you a whole lot about physical science!

Road Runner
(Speedius birdius)

Coyote
(Hungrius carnivorii)

CLANG!

by MARK WEAKLAND
illustrated by LOIC BILLIAU

WILE E. COYOTE
EXPERIMENTS WITH
MAGNETISM

Magnets Attract!

Poor Wile E. Coyote. He tries so hard to attract success, but all he gets is trouble. Maybe Wile E. should study the science of magnets. If he understood what they are and how they work, catching Road Runner might not be so painful.

Coyote
(Hungrius carnivorii)

Road Runner
(Speedius birdius)

A magnet is any object that produces an invisible **magnetic field**. Some magnets are shaped like bars. Some are shaped like horseshoes. Some magnets are small and some are large. A magnet's magnetic field **attracts** certain substances. But a feather is not one of them. No matter the size or shape, a magnet will never attract a bird. But a steel sign? Yes!

magnetic field—a region of space near a magnet or electric current in which a magnetic force can act on an object

attract—to pull something toward something else

9

Lodestones

Most magnets are manufactured, but a few occur in nature. These natural magnets are called lodestones. Lodestones can be found in rocks lying on the ground. Wile E. is learning about them the hard way.

Magnets are made of metal. Most are made of iron. Heavy and gray, iron is the most commonly found metal on Earth. Iron is found in many places, including rocks.

Scientists think lightning could create lodestones. A bolt of lightning produces a strong electric current. The current creates a powerful magnetic field. If a rock is struck by lightning, it comes in contact with the magnetic field. The iron in the rock would be permanently magnetized. This would create a natural magnet.

Lodestones can be hard to find. But Wile E. has found one. What a lucky coyote!

Magnets and Iron

Magnetic force attracts all kinds of objects. Wile E. learned this when his magnet pulled that road sign out of the ground. The sign was made of steel, which is a blend of iron and other metals.

IRON BBs
ACME

BIRD SEED +
IRON BBs

BIRD SEED
ACME

Magnets don't attract everything. They won't attract wooden pencils, plastic toys, gold bracelets, or silver chains. But they will attract objects made with iron. Metal desks, refrigerator doors, nails, paper clips, and steel BBs all contain iron. Too bad those BBs aren't inside Road Runner!

Magnetic Fields

A magnet's power comes from its invisible magnetic field. The field produces the force that pushes and pulls on objects. But if the field is invisible, how can Wile E. be sure it is there?

ACME
IRON FILINGS

ACME
BIG BAR MAGNET

BIG BAR
MAGNET

GIANT SKILLET   FIRE PIT

To see the magnetic field around his magnet, Wile E. scatters small pieces of iron. These tiny iron flakes are called iron filings. The filings line up in the direction of the magnetic field. Filings make it possible to see how the invisible field surrounds the magnet.

There is a lot of force coming from this magnet. Wile E. thinks it's strong enough to pull his iron skillet into the fire. Let's find out if he's right.

ACME
IRON FILINGS

BIG BAR
MAGNET

CHAPTER 2

OPPOSITES ATTRACT

Magnetic Poles

Magnets have **polarity**. Polarity means there are two things opposing each other. A magnet's power is strongest at its two ends. This is easy to see in a bar magnet, which is a straight piece of magnetized iron.

The two ends of a bar magnet are called **poles**. They are typically named the north pole and the south pole.

Wile E. plans to use his magnet to pull Road Runner. Will his plan work?

Earth is like a giant magnet. It has a solid iron core in the center that is surrounded by hot liquid rock, which also contains iron. As the iron in the liquid rock moves around the iron core, a magnetic field is created. Like all magnets, Earth has a north and south pole. Earth's magnetic north pole points toward the south. The magnetic south pole points toward the north.

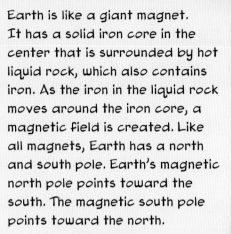

polarity—having two oppositely charged poles; one end of a magnet is called the north pole and the other end is called the south pole

pole—either of the two regions or parts of a magnet that exhibits magnetic polarity

Poles Attract and Repel

Magnets can attract or **repel**. Opposite poles of a magnet attract. A north pole attracts a south pole. Poor Wile E. is experiencing that right now!

repel—to exert a force on an object so that the object is pushed away

Matching poles repel each other. A south pole repels another south pole. In fact, it's almost impossible to make them touch! It looks like Wile E.'s life would be easier with magnets that repel instead of attract.

Magnets Repel Iron

Wile E. is discovering that any iron object can become magnetized if it comes in contact with a strong magnet.

To make a magnet, start with a nail. Let the magnet attract the nail. Then let the nail and magnet sit overnight. When the magnet and nail are separated, the nail will have some magnetic force. This means the nail will attract and repel other magnets. Likewise, one end of a real magnet will attract the nail. The other will repel it. Wile E. magnetized his dart this way.

DART

Wile E.'s plan might have worked if the Road Runner hadn't ducked. But he did. Plus, Wile E. forgot about the iron fire hydrant. Now his plan for capturing Road Runner is all washed up!

CHAPTER 3

AN ELECTRIFYING EXPERIENCE

Electricity and Magnetism

With his glasses and big book, Wile E. looks pretty smart right now. He is reading all about electricity and magnetism. Wile E. is learning that they are a lot alike. Check out his chart that compares the two.

Electricity	Magnetism
positive and negative charges	north and south poles
opposite charges attract	opposite poles attract
matching charges repel	matching poles repel
fields form around the charges	fields form around the poles
electric field comes from charges	magnetic field comes from moving charges

Because electricity and magnetism are related, Wile E. can make a special magnet. It's called an **electromagnet.** For a genius like Wile E., making one is easy. All he needs is wire, electricity, and a quiet place to work.

electromagnet—a device consisting of an iron or steel core that is magnetized by an electric current in a coil that surrounds it

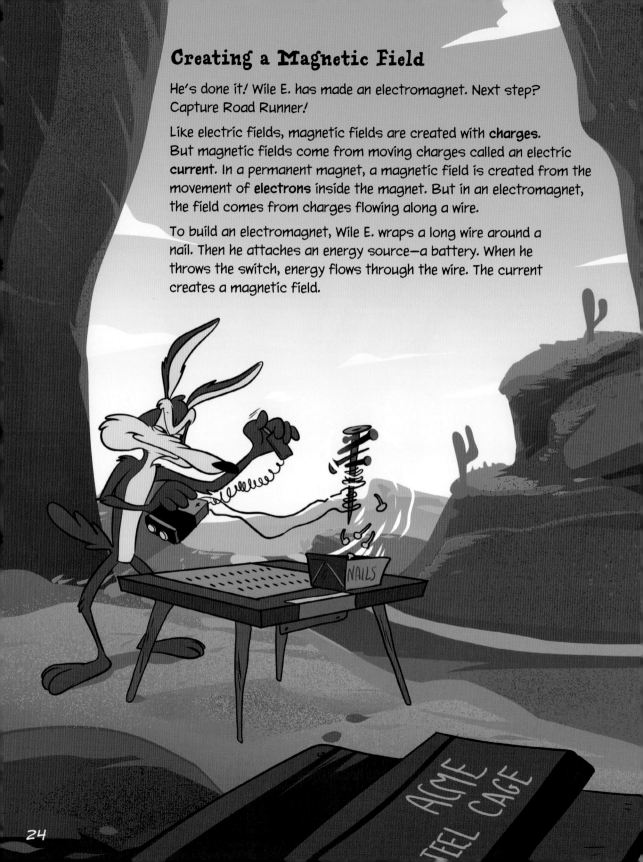

Creating a Magnetic Field

He's done it! Wile E. has made an electromagnet. Next step? Capture Road Runner!

Like electric fields, magnetic fields are created with **charges**. But magnetic fields come from moving charges called an electric **current**. In a permanent magnet, a magnetic field is created from the movement of **electrons** inside the magnet. But in an electromagnet, the field comes from charges flowing along a wire.

To build an electromagnet, Wile E. wraps a long wire around a nail. Then he attaches an energy source—a battery. When he throws the switch, energy flows through the wire. The current creates a magnetic field.

With his switch, Wile E. can turn his magnet on and off. What magnet tricks will he perform next?

charge—the amount of electricity moving through something
current—the flow of electric charges
electron—one of the tiny particles that make up all things

Electromagnets

Wile E.'s magnet gun is made from wire wrapped
around an iron bar. When a current flows through
the wire, a magnetic field forms around the wire.
This magnetizes the iron bar. Now it acts like a
magnet. The strength of the magnetic field depends
on the number of coils in the wire.

To build a strong magnet, Wile E. wraps the wire around and around the bar.
Now he hopes to pull anything metal to him, even a heavy steel cage.

Wait a minute ... nothing is happening. It looks like Wile E.'s magnet gun isn't strong enough. To fix the problem, he could add more wire. He could add more electricity. Or he could do both. More wire and more electricity will certainly make Wile E.'s magnet more powerful.

More Electromagnets

Wile E.'s small magnet gun wasn't strong enough to attract the cage. But his new, giant magnet gun should do the trick.

More powerful electromagnets can be made by wrapping lots of wire. But more than wire is needed. To make a magnet as powerful as possible, an electric current is needed. Lots of it. When more electric current flows, a stronger magnetic field is created.

Powerful electromagnets attract all kinds of iron objects. In a scrapyard, an electromagnet can lift more than 2,000 pounds (907 kilograms) of scrap metal at a time.

Wile E.'s magnet is working well—too well. Poor Wile E.! He fails even when he succeeds.

Magnets in Motors

It's up, up, and away. To capture Road Runner, Wile E. is test-driving his new electric motor flying machine.

Electric motors are everywhere. They spin ceiling fans, power toy trains, and turn the beaters on electric mixers. Inside each motor is a set of magnets. Each magnet generates a magnetic field. The two fields attract and repel one another in a constant cycle. This cycle can be turned into motion. Here's how:

Wile E. wraps a **rotor** in wire. A current flows through the wire, creating a magnetic field. A magnet is on both sides of the rotor. Each magnet's poles alternately attract and repel each other. This makes the rotor spin on its axle.

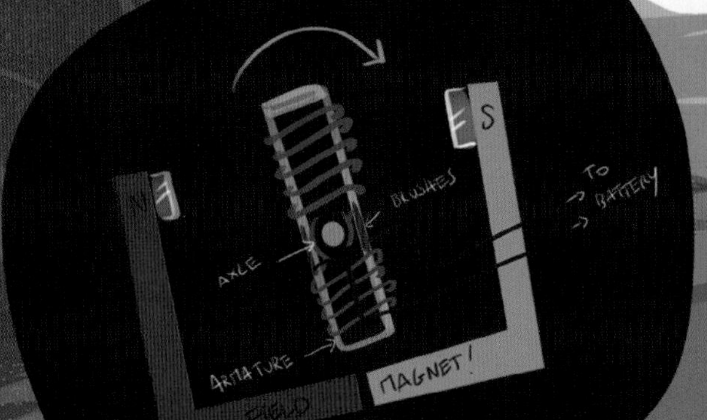

S

TO BATTERY

BRUSHES

AXLE

ARMATURE

FIELD

MAGNET!

rotor—a rotating part of a machine

A motor's spinning axle does a lot of work. Attach beaters to it, and the motor will mix brownie batter. Put helicopter rotors on it, and the motor will lift a coyote into the air. But Wile E. has forgotten one important thing—electric motors only run when there is electricity!

Magnets Matter

Wile E.'s magnetic plans never worked. Road Runner is still on the loose, racing up and down the roads. And Wile E. is still chasing Road Runner with his knife and fork.

Even though his plans failed, Wile E. learned a lot about magnets. Now he knows they attract and repel objects made of iron. He knows that all magnets have a magnetic field and two poles, one north and one south. And Wile E. understands that magnetism is related to electricity. Because the two are related, wire and electricity can be used to make an electromagnet.

Maybe Road Runner is like a magnet. Why else would Wile E. Coyote be so attracted to him?

KABOOOM!

WILE E. COYOTE EXPERIMENTS WITH CHEMICAL REACTIONS

by MARK WEAKLAND   illustrated by LOIC BILLIAU

React!

Being a genius is a tough job. For all his brainpower, Wile E. Coyote can never get rid of that Road Runner. Maybe it's because Wile E. doesn't understand the science behind all of his tricks.

Coyote
(Hungrius carnivorii)

Road Runner
(Speedius birdius)

CLICK

Take **chemical reactions,** for example. Wile E. is trying to use chemistry to defeat Road Runner. He wants to create a gas that will lift the balloon. The rising balloon will strike a match and fire a rocket. BOOM! Road Runner will be toast.

But Wile E.'s plan is doomed to fail. If he knew more about chemical reactions, he'd know why his machine isn't working. And he could make one that worked.

chemical reaction—a process in which one or more substances are made into a new substance or substances

37

Wile E. is surrounded by chemical reactions. They cause his bread to rise. They make his cleansers work. They digest the food in his belly. Every time Wile E. lights a fire or browns meat in a skillet, he starts a chemical reaction.

Kitchen Classics
R R STEW
4 c. of water
1 tsp. of salt
1 FROZEN ROAD RUNNER
2 POTATOES

Not everything is a chemical reaction. A piece of bread turning to toast is a reaction. But a giant pot of water growing hotter and hotter is not. Wile E. is hoping to freeze Road Runner for his stew. Would that be a chemical reaction? Let's find out.

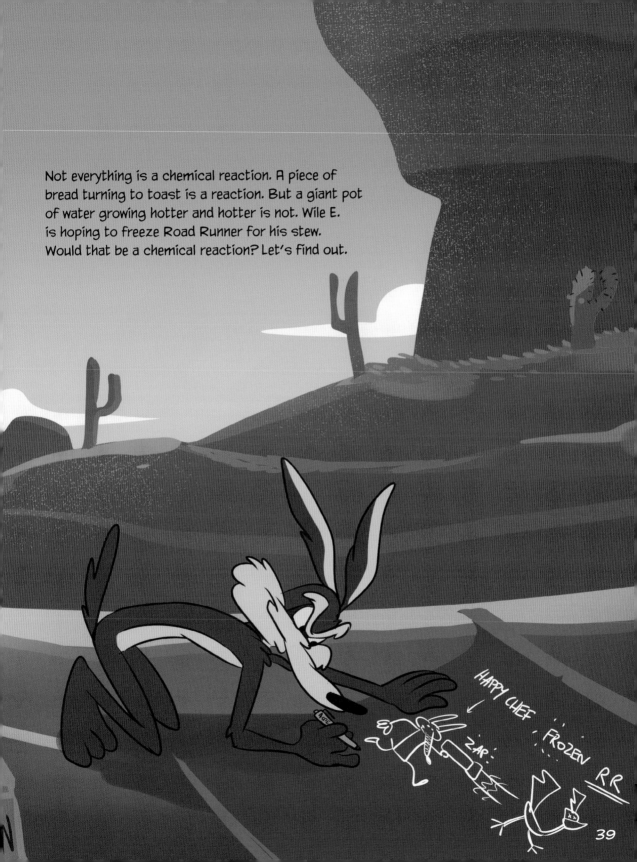

HAPPY CHEF FROZEN RR

ZAP!

CHAPTER 1

THE ELEMENTS OF MATTER

Everything Is Matter

Wile E. needs one frozen Road Runner to make his stew. And he needs to understand **matter** to make his chemical reactions work. Unfortunately, Wile E. is having trouble getting either one!

Everything is made of matter, including water, soup, and coyotes. Matter exists in one of three forms: solid, liquid, or gas. When solid ice melts, its form changes to liquid. When water boils into steam, its form changes to gas. But these changes are not chemical reactions. Water is still water, even when it changes form. Chemical reactions occur only when substances are changed into entirely new substances.

Speaking of reactions, look at Road Runner.
He thinks this change is hilarious!

matter—particles of which everything
in the universe is made

Wile E. knows all about winter. He knows that salt melts snow and ice. But does he know that snow, ice, and salt are made of **atoms**?

Matter's basic building blocks are tiny things called atoms. There are more than 100 different kinds of atoms. Each kind is called an **element**. Elements are often organized in the Periodic Table of Elements.

When atoms stick together, it's called bonding. Atoms bond because they are attracted to one another. When one atom bonds to another, a **molecule** is formed.

atom—a tiny particle of which everything is made

element—a basic substance that is made up of only one kind of atom

molecule—the atoms making up the smallest unit of a substance; H_2O is a molecule of water

A **compound** is a substance that forms when different kinds of atoms bond together. For example, salt is not made from salt atoms. Salt is made from one atom of sodium and one atom of chlorine. Sodium and chlorine are elements. When the atoms of these elements bond, they form a new substance—salt! Salt's chemical name is sodium chloride, or NaCl.

PROTON

ELECTRON

NUCLEUS

NEUTRON

Atoms are made up of electrons, protons, and neutrons. In the middle of the atom is the nucleus. This is where the protons and neutrons hang out. Electrons are found in the outer part of the atom.

compound—a substance made of two or more elements bonded together

CHAPTER 2

CHEMISTRY SET

Reagents and Products

Wile E. hopes to use vinegar and baking soda to blow up Road Runner. Will his plan work? Let's learn more about his chemical reaction and find out.

Reagents are the substances used to make chemical reactions. In Wile E.'s plan, vinegar is one reagent. Baking soda is another. Reagents come together and react to make a new substance, or **product**. Wile E.'s two reagents will come together and make carbon dioxide gas, or CO_2. CO_2 is a compound formed when one atom of carbon bonds with two atoms of oxygen.

reagent—a substance that takes part in and undergoes change during a reaction

product—something that is made

Wile E. thinks this CO_2 gas will erupt into a giant explosion. Could this finally be the end of Road Runner?

ACME
BAKING SODA

ACME VINEGAR

Reaction Rate

Wile is learning that not all chemical reactions occur at the same rate. Some reactions happen quickly, such as an explosion. Others take a long time, such as metal rusting. Reagents turn into products at a certain speed. This speed is called the **reaction rate**.

When energy is added to a reaction, the reaction rate changes. The added energy could be from heat, sunlight, or electricity.

HERE!

MAKE A DESERT SNOWBALL!

FUN!

PFFT

reaction rate—how fast or slow a reaction takes place

ACME BAKING SODA

ACME VINEG

The reaction rate also changes when more or less of the reagents are used. This is why Wile E.'s first plan fizzled out. He only added a little vinegar to the baking soda. That only made a little carbon dioxide.

Wile E.'s second plan blew up in his face. Why? He added too much vinegar. The baking soda dissolved quickly, so the reagents reacted quickly.

CHAPTER 3

LIGHTS, CAMERAS, REACTION!

Activation Energy

There are many types of chemical reactions. One type combines two substances to make a third substance.

Wile E. wants to use water to wash away Road Runner. Too bad he's out of water. But Wile E. has a plan—he'll make his own! Wile E. knows water is a compound made from one oxygen molecule and two hydrogen molecules. But simply mixing hydrogen and oxygen molecules together won't work. Why? Not all substances react when you put them together. Putting hydrogen with oxygen just makes a big cloud of these gases.

Often, adding energy gets a reaction going. This is called **activation energy**. In his second try, Wile E. added energy by striking a match. What a dangerous thing to do! Hydrogen gas catches fire in the blink of an eye. And oxygen makes things burn fast. Hydrogen and oxygen atoms make water molecules when energy is added. But the water is created through an explosion.

activation energy—the least amount of energy required to activate atoms or molecules to a state in which they can undergo a chemical reaction

Iron Oxide

Wile E. has a towering plan for catching Road Runner. But a chemical reaction is about to spoil it. Poor Wile E.!

Rusting is another type of chemical reaction. When iron comes in contact with oxygen in the presence of water, iron oxide forms. This is also called rust.

Wile E. has already learned that reaction rates can speed up or slow down. But he didn't learn his lesson very well. He hasn't noticed that the iron tower is rusting quickly. Paint and oil keep iron from coming in contact with oxygen in the air. But the legs of the tower have no paint or oil on them. Iron oxide also forms more quickly in wet places. Two of the tower legs are planted in marshy soil!

Next time Wile E. should think more carefully about reaction rates. But right now he's only thinking about the ground!

Combustion

Burning is another chemical reaction. Right now Wile E. is burning gasoline in the engine of his race car.

Burning is called **combustion**. It is a reaction that produces energy in the form of heat. Combustion occurs when oxygen combines with fuel. There are many types of fuel. In a campfire, wood is the fuel. In a candle flame, wax is the fuel. And in Wile E.'s race car, gasoline is the fuel.

When a fuel and oxygen react, two products are created—water and carbon dioxide. Fuel such as oil and coal are "dirty." They produce other products as well, such as soot.

Combustion reactions make trucks, cars, trains, and airplanes go. These reactions occur when energy is added to oxygen and fuel. In an engine, spark plugs provide energy. It doesn't take much, just one little spark. But without a spark, Wile E. isn't going anywhere!

SPARK PLUGS

BUMP BUMP

combustion—burning; a fast chemical change that occurs when oxygen combines with another substance

Combustion and Oxidizers

Wile E. loves rockets even more than race cars. Look at him go!

Like cars, rockets are propelled by a combustion reaction. The combustion requires fuel and a source of oxygen. In rockets, the fuel is often liquid hydrogen. The source of oxygen is called the **oxidizer**. In a rocket, the oxidizer is liquid oxygen.

oxidizer—a chemical that a fuel requires to burn

Some type of heat starts the combustion. For his rocket, Wile E. uses a lit fuse. Heat starts combustion, but heat is also a product of combustion. In other words, burning begins with heat. The burning also produces heat. The produced heat creates even more burning.

This cycle of heat, burning, and more heat is why combustion reactions happen very quickly. After combustion starts, additional heat is not needed to keep it going. As Wile E. is finding out, combustion is like a wildfire. Once it starts, it is difficult to stop!

BLAM!

CHAPTER 4

REACTIONS INSIDE AND OUT

Catalyst

To catch Road Runner, Wile E. needs more than fancy shoes. He needs chemical reactions. Lots of them!

Inside his body, millions of chemical reactions are happening every minute. They happen in his lungs and in his muscles. They even happen in his brain. Without chemical reactions, Wile E. couldn't even think about catching Road Runner.

Chemical reactions outside of the body often need high heat to get started. Think of a match lighting a fire. But reactions inside the body start without a match. And they operate at low temperatures.

Chemical reactions inside Wile E.'s body use **catalysts**. Catalysts are substances that lower the amount of energy needed for reactions to start. They also speed up reactions, even at low temperatures.

The catalysts inside Wile E. are called **enzymes**. They help protect his body from harmful temperatures. And enzymes let reactions occur at Wile E.'s body temperature, which is 100 degrees Fahrenheit (38 degrees Celsius). There's no need to sweat it when catalysts are on your side.

FOOSH!

catalyst—a substance that speeds up a chemical reaction without being used up by the chemical reaction

enzyme—a special protein that speeds up chemical reactions in the body

Explosion

What's one of Wile E.'s favorite plans for getting rid of his enemy? A stick of dynamite and a giant explosion! But if he isn't careful, he'll only blow up himself.

Wile E.'s stick of dynamite is a solid chemical fuel. A burning fuse provides the heat energy to start the reaction. During an explosion, reacting materials create gases. These gases create pressure around the reaction. The added energy from the pressure causes the chemical reaction to go very quickly. The total reaction time can be a millionth of a second or less.

WOOSH!

During an explosion a shock wave rushes out at **supersonic** speed. This wave can cause a lot of damage. Explosions knock down walls, blow craters in the earth, and launch coyotes into the air. What has four legs, fur, and flies? A coyote, of course!

The shock wave from an explosion can travel as fast as 22,000 miles (35,406 kilometers) per hour. Temperatures in an explosion reach more than 9,000 degrees F (4,982 degrees C).

KABOOM!!

supersonic—faster than the speed of sound

Wile E. has learned a lot about chemical reactions. He knows chemical reactions are more than matter changing form. He knows that chemical reactions create new substances. He also knows that burning and rusting are types of reactions. And Wile E. knows that a burst of energy can start a reaction.

At the beginning, a lack of energy is why Wile E.'s machine didn't work. It needed a spark. But in the end, poor Wile E. has forgotten the most important thing. He forgot that in a chemical reaction, a spark can lead to an explosion.

Wile E. Coyote

Experiments with

SIMPLE MACHINES

by
Mark Weakland

illustrated by
Christian Cornia

Introduction:

A Better Way to Work

Catching a Road Runner is hard work. There are rocks to move, **anvils** to lift, and holes to dig. But no matter how hard Wile E. Coyote works, he never manages to catch that crafty bird. Wile E. wouldn't have to work so hard if he learned to correctly use simple machines. The six types of simple machines include levers, wheels and axles, pulleys, inclined planes, wedges, and screws.

Road Runner
(Speedius birdius)

When Wile E. exerts a force to lift a rock or dig a hole, he does work. In science, work is defined as the effort or force needed to move an object over a certain distance. Using simple machines would make Wile E.'s work much easier. Why? Because simple machines reduce the amount of force he needs to move something. If he pushed a lever or pulled a rope on a pulley, the same work would be done with a lot less force. Learn how to use simple machines, Wile E.! Your work will be easier, and you might have more luck catching Road Runner too!

anvil—a large steel block with a flat top

Coyote
(Hungrius carnivorii)

Chapter 1: Whatever the Lever

Levers and Fulcrums

A deep pit makes a good Road Runner trap. But digging is hard work. And Wile E. isn't strong enough to lift a big stone out of his hole.

A simple lever can help Wile E. solve his problem. A lever is a bar that turns against a resting point called a **fulcrum**. To make a lever, Wile E. first jams one end of a pry bar under the big rock. Then he places a smaller rock under the bar to be the fulcrum.

With the lever, Wile E. can lift a heavy **load** like the big rock with much less effort. But he needs to place the fulcrum in the correct spot. If it's too close to him, the lever moves only a short distance when he pushes on it. It barely affects the rock.

But if Wile E. places the fulcrum closer to the big rock, the lever moves over a greater distance. This creates a large force on the other end of the pry bar. But be careful, Wile E.! If you exert too much force, it can lead to unexpected—and painful—results!

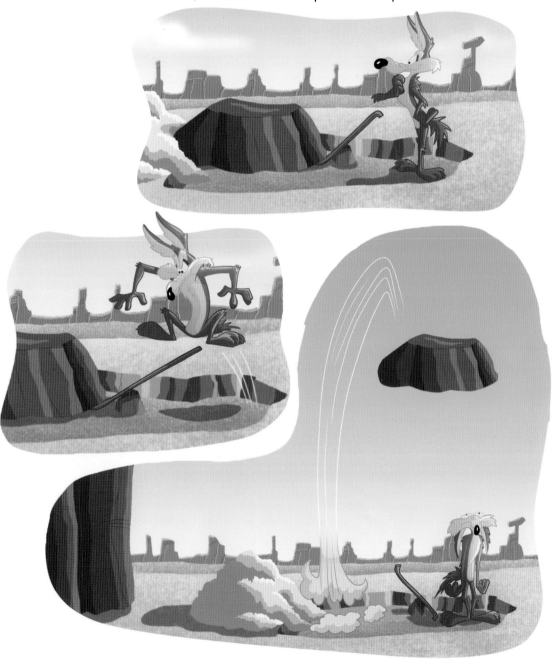

fulcrum—a resting point on which a lever pivots
load—an object that moves when a force is applied

Input and Output Forces

Wile E. has learned that flying rocks can be hard on the head. Now he'd like to launch a boulder at Road Runner. But how can he throw it accurately? His ACME catapult should get the job done!

Wile E.'s catapult is a lever made with a sturdy bar and a fulcrum. Like all levers, it involves two separate forces. An input force is applied to the lever to move a load. The output force is the result of the lever acting on the load. For example, a strong spring provides input force on the catapult's arm, which turns on a fulcrum. This results in a strong output force that launches the boulder through the air.

WHUMP!

What Wile E. doesn't know is that sometimes an output force from one system can act as an input force for another. When his catapult flings the boulder, it causes another to come hurtling back at him. Look out, Wile E.!

OUCH!

Chapter 2: Inclined to Fail

Planes and Ramps

Looks like Wile E. still plans to crush Road Runner with a heavy object. But he's having trouble getting that big log to the top of the canyon wall. Luckily for him, there's more than one way to move a heavy object.

A plane is any flat surface, such as a smooth board lying flat on the ground. Unfortunately, a flat plane isn't very useful for making work easier. However, Wile E. can create a simple machine by lifting one end of the plane. Like other simple machines, inclined planes reduce the effort needed to move a heavy load.

RAMP LOG ME

Wile E. doesn't need to lift the log up a short distance. Instead, he can simply roll it up a ramp, which is a type of inclined plane. The ramp allows Wile E. to exert a smaller force over a longer distance. The result is the same—the heavy log moves to a new height. Only this time Wile E. doesn't have to work as hard.

Of course, it would have been better if he had built his ramp strong enough to support the log's weight!

Moving from High to Low

Can a coyote catch a roadrunner with a ski jump? Wile E. thinks so, and he's about to find out!

Inclined planes are useful for moving something from a low point to a high point. But they also help do the opposite. Wile E.'s ski jump quickly moves him from a high point to a low point. If he uses it correctly, he should easily catch Road Runner.

But Wile E. should also remember that the force of **gravity** constantly pulls objects toward the ground. Gravity quickly pulls loose objects down a ramp.

SMAK!

Pulled by gravity, Wile E. zooms down the ramp. Uh-oh. It looks like Wile E. didn't think about how much gravity would affect him. Too much speed caused him to have too much distance on his jump. You overshot your target Wile E.!

gravity—a force that pulls objects with mass together

The Wedge

Wile E. has tried rolling logs and flinging boulders with catapults. But he hasn't had any luck in squashing Road Runner. He's got another idea to try, though. Maybe a rolling boulder will get the job done.

To release the boulder, Wile E. uses an axe to cut through a rope. An axe is a type of simple machine called a wedge. A wedge is made of two inclined planes that come together to a point on one side. Wedges are usually made of a strong material like wood or steel. Doorstops, chisels, and axes are all examples of wedges.

Like all simple machines, wedges do work. Their pointed ends can enter tight places and are good for pushing things apart. Doorstops can prop open doors. Chisels can split apart stone and cement. And axes are good at chopping through rope and wood.

After cutting the rope, Wile E. sees that a cactus is in the way. So he uses his wedge-shaped axe to chop it down. Unfortunately, he didn't think to place some other wedges under the boulder first. They could have kept the boulder from flattening him!

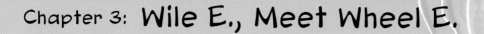

Chapter 3: Wile E., Meet Wheel E.

Rotational Motion of Wheels and Axles

Wile E.'s efforts have given him a headache instead of a tasty dinner. But he's hoping his wheeled wagon will provide a less painful way to squash that pesky Road Runner.

A wheel and axle is a simple machine that produces **rotational motion**. This motion can be used for doing work, such as moving heavy boulders. Wile E.'s wagon rests on top of two axles. When he pushes on it, the wheels turn and the wagon moves, along with anything sitting on it.

WHEEL   AXLE

Wheels and axles are simple machines that make life easier for everyone, including coyotes. With his wheeled wagon, Wile E. can move a giant boulder with just a push of his paw. However, wagons and boulders weigh a lot, and some rock ledges aren't very strong. Poor Wile E., here comes another headache!

rotational motion—the motion of an object rotating around a fixed point

Rotational vs. Straight-Line Motion

Wile E. has had trouble using a catapult and a wheeled vehicle by themselves. But what if he tried using them together? Armed with a catapult on a wagon, Wile E. sets out to crush Road Runner. He just has to get his machine into position. What could possibly go wrong?

Wheels and axles help create straight-line motion. When wheels are attached to vehicles, their rotational motion is transferred to the vehicles through the axles. This motion in turn causes the vehicles to move in a straight line. Any objects carried by the vehicles also move in a straight line. Wheeled vehicles can carry heavy loads in a straight line over long distances.

Of course, wheeled vehicles need to be kept under control. If they aren't, they can roll away and cause a lot of problems. Too bad Wile E. overlooked this fact. Now he's the one about to get crushed!

SPROING!

Chapter 4: Pull Me, Pull E.

The Pulley

To pull off his latest plan, Wile E. needs to get to the top of a platform. But how can he get himself up there? Using his scrawny arms and legs to climb up would be a lot of work. Why not use a simple machine like a pulley to do the job?

Pulleys are simple machines that make raising and lowering loads much easier. Wile E.'s pulley uses a rope and a grooved wheel. The wheel rotates around an axle. The rotational motion of the pulley causes the rope to move either up or down. Wile E. can use the wheel's motion to raise and lower objects, including himself.

A pulley makes work easier by changing the direction of force that Wile E. needs to apply to the rope. If he pulled up on a rope without a pulley, he'd be working against gravity. But if he uses a pulley, he can work with gravity instead. When he pulls down on one side, the other side moves up. Wile E.'s pulley can help him get to the top of the platform quickly and easily. But he didn't expect Road Runner to be at the top!

Reducing Applied Force

Dropping rocks from a high ledge hasn't worked well for Wile E. This time he thinks an anvil might work better. But pulling an anvil up to the top of a ledge is difficult. Wile E. knows that a pulley can help lift objects. Unfortunately, one pulley isn't enough to get his heavy anvil up to the rock ledge. What if he tries using more than one?

Using multiple pulleys makes work easier because they reduce the force needed to lift heavy objects. If Wile E. uses two pulleys, he can use half as much force to lift the anvil. Using three pulleys would reduce his effort to one-third of what he needed before. And with four pulleys, Wile E. would need to use just one-fourth of the force.

However, applied forces and distance always balance out. Pulleys greatly reduce the amount of force Wile E. uses to lift the anvil. But he has to pull a lot more rope to achieve his goal.

Oops! Wile E. missed one small detail. He didn't need to keep walking backward with the rope. He could have stayed in one spot to hoist the anvil up. Looks like he'll be hanging around for a while until he figures out a new plan.

Chapter 5: Spiraling Out of Control

Screws

Wile E. hasn't had much luck so far. But he would still love to crush Road Runner under a big rock. His latest idea is to use a jack to do some heavy lifting for him.

Jacks are complex machines. But the main part of a jack is a simple machine called a screw. A screw is an inclined plane that is wrapped around a **cylinder**. Its spiraling edge is very useful for doing difficult tasks.

cylinder—a shape with flat, circular ends and sides shaped like a tube

Screws are usually used for holding things together, such as two pieces of wood or a lid on a jar. But screws are also useful for raising and lowering heavy objects. When the screw in a jack turns, a platform moves up or down along the screw's inclined plane.

While a screw can help make lifting objects easier, turning it can be difficult. Wile E. can make his job even easier by using a motor to turn the screw. But he's got to be careful! A motorized screw can get out of control. Wile E. should learn that sometimes it's better to just do the work by hand.

Screws Convert Rotational Motion

Dropping anvils and boulders from a high ledge hasn't worked well for Wile E. So instead he's going to try dropping the ledge itself—by blasting it with dynamite! But first Wile E. needs to drill a hole into the rock to hold the explosives.

Like wheels and axles, screws can change rotational motion into other types of motion. Augers are large motorized screws used for drilling holes into the earth. The rotational motion of the motor turns the auger. As the auger turns, its spiraling edges move it down into the rock. Soon the screw-shaped auger creates a hole.

Uh-oh! Looks like Wile E.'s machine got stuck on some extra hard rock. The motor's rotational motion was shifted to Wile E. instead of the auger. The fast spinning motion sent him flying over the cliff's edge. Sometimes nothing seems to go right, even for a "Super Genius" like Wile E.

Simple Machines to the Rescue

Wile E. hasn't had much success in getting Road Runner. But simple machines have played an important part in his schemes. From moving boulders to drilling holes, simple machines have helped Wile E. do a lot of work.

pulley

wheel and axle

screw

wedge

inclined plane

lever

Simple machines are important for other reasons too. More complicated machines are often made from combining simple machines. Bicycles and bulldozers use a combination of levers, wheels and axles, pulleys, and more. Without simple machines, many machines in our world would not exist. We wouldn't be able to build roads and buildings, drive cars, or explore space without the help of simple machines.

Will Wile E. ever be able to capture Road Runner? Only time will tell. Although he hasn't had much luck, he'll keep trying. If Wile E. ever catches that sneaky bird, chances are good that a simple machine will help him finally succeed.

Wile E. Coyote
Experiments with
STATES of MATTER

by Suzanne Slade

illustrated by
Christian Cornia

Introduction:
Matter All Around

Wile E. Coyote can't seem to get a break. No matter how hard he tries, he can't catch that speedy Road Runner. The problem is, Wile E. keeps forgetting the ways that matter all around him can change.

Coyote
(Hungrius carnivorii)

Everything Wile E. can see and touch is made of matter. The mountains, sand, snow, and even that tasty Road Runner are matter. Matter is made of tiny **atoms** and **molecules** that are too small to see.

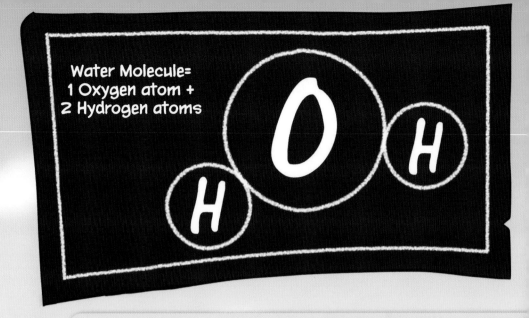

**Water Molecule=
1 Oxygen atom +
2 Hydrogen atoms**

Matter takes up space and has **mass**. It can also change state, or be changed into different types of matter. If Wile E. wants to catch Road Runner, he needs to learn more about matter. If he does, maybe he'll understand why the way matter changes its state often ruins his plans.

atom—an element in its smallest form
molecule—a group of two or more atoms bonded together
mass—the amount of material in an object

Road Runner
(Speedius birdius)

The States of Matter

If Wile E. looked around, he'd notice that there are four types of matter—solids, liquids, gases, and plasma. Each type acts differently and has its own physical **properties**.

solid

gas

liquid

SPLASH

• **Solids:** Solids hold their shape and fill a certain amount of space. The solid ground can support Wile E. as he zooms after Road Runner.

• **Gases:** Gases move freely. They have no fixed shape and take up whatever space is available. Air is a gas that moves and flows around Wile E. When he flies off a cliff, he falls through the air to the ground below.

• **Liquids:** Liquids also fill a certain amount of space. But they don't hold their shape. They can move and flow. When Wile E. lands in the river, liquid water flows around him as he sinks.

• **Plasma:** Plasma is made of highly charged atoms or molecules. The sun and stars are made up of plasma. It is rarely found on Earth because high temperatures are needed to maintain it.

plasma

Poor Wile E.! It looks like his plan failed. Will this old coyote ever learn some new tricks? Let's take a peek at his newest schemes and see why his ideas never seem to work.

property—a quality of a material, such as color, hardness, or shape

Chapter 1:
Properties of the States of Matter

Solids

Wile E. isn't the world's greatest artist. But this hungry coyote can paint a pretty good desert scene. With a little paint and a solid board, he's sure his new plan will stop Road Runner in his tracks.

In a solid object, molecules are arranged close together. The tightly packed molecules make the object hard and help it keep its shape. Wile E. knows that his hard, solid board will stop Road Runner's speedy ways.

MOLECULES IN SOLID

But Wile E. has overlooked one little detail. Solids don't change shape on their own. However, a strong outside force can change a solid's shape. When Wile E.'s dynamite explodes, its energy breaks the solid rock ledge above him. Too bad he didn't think of that before setting up his trap. Ouch!

Liquids

Wile E. knows that Road Runner likes a refreshing swim on a hot day. With his new plan, Wile E. hopes Road Runner will take a dip in his cool pool. Then he'll use his ACME Instant-Glue powder to capture that speedy bird.

When Wile E. turns on the faucet, liquid water moves quickly through a hose to fill up the pool. Liquid molecules easily move and flow around each other through pipes and hoses. Liquids also take the shape of their containers. Eventually, the water fills up the round pool.

ROAD RUNNER RESORT

ACME INSTANT GLUE

JUST ADD WATER

WATER MOLECULES

Get ready Wile E. Road Runner is about to jump into your trap. Oops! Wile E. forgot an important detail about liquids. Unlike solids, liquid molecules don't hold together tightly. When Road Runner jumped in the pool, the water easily flowed out and splashed on him. Unfortunately, when Wile E.'s glue got wet it became a thick, sticky liquid. That coyote has gotten himself into one sticky situation this time!

Gas Molecules

Gases

Wile E.'s new plan uses a balloon filled with **helium** gas for a sneaky air attack. With luck, Wile E. hopes that pesky bird will never see the heavy anvil falling out of the sky.

Both liquids and gases are **fluids**. They flow and take the shape of the container that holds them. For example, the helium gas in Wile E.'s tank takes the shape of the cylinder. When he fills the balloon, the gas molecules spread out and take the shape of the round balloon. Helium gas is lighter than air. Soon the gas fills the balloon enough to lift Wile E. and his anvil into the air.

Wile E. is on his way, but wants to go faster. The helium gas pushes against the balloon's walls and creates **pressure** inside. Wile E. thinks filling the balloon with more helium will help him fly faster to catch Road Runner. But he doesn't realize that containers can only take a certain amount of pressure—more isn't always better. Wait Wile E., that's too much!

BOOM

Oops! The pressure inside the balloon went beyond its breaking point. Unfortunately for Wile E., the air is made up of gas molecules too. It's not able to support coyotes, or their anvils. Better luck next time, Wile E.!

helium—a light, colorless gas that does not burn
fluid—a liquid or gas substance that flows
pressure—the amount of force over a certain area

Plasma

Wile E. has another high-flying plan to catch Road Runner. This time he's taking to the skies in a new "Triple-Strength" ACME balloon. He's not going to let anything stop him this time, especially a little rainstorm. But Wile E. shouldn't ignore the fourth state of matter—plasma.

Plasma is different from other states of matter. It only exists at very high temperatures and is full of tiny particles called free electrons. These free electrons can move easily between atoms. This movement causes the matter in plasma to become highly charged and it starts to glow.

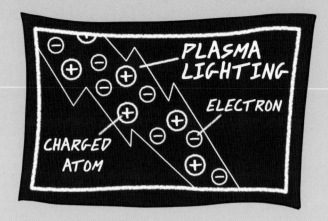

Plasma is the most common type of matter in the universe. It is found in the Sun and in every star. But plasma is rarely found on Earth. Neon and fluorescent lightbulbs use plasma to create light. And as Wile E. has learned, plasma also exists on Earth as lightning. Because it is highly charged, it's attracted to metal objects, such as anvils. Looks like Wile E. will be seeing stars for a while!

Chapter 2: Changing States of Matter

Freeze Frame

Wile E. thinks he has the perfect plan to get Road Runner this time. With his ACME Freeze Ray, he's sure he can stop that speedy bird in his tracks. But to make sure it works, he's testing it first on a powerful waterfall.

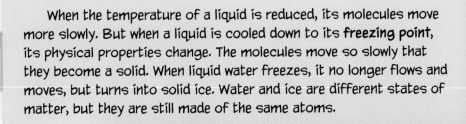

When the temperature of a liquid is reduced, its molecules move more slowly. But when a liquid is cooled down to its **freezing point**, its physical properties change. The molecules move so slowly that they become a solid. When liquid water freezes, it no longer flows and moves, but turns into solid ice. Water and ice are different states of matter, but they are still made of the same atoms.

Could Wile E.'s crafty plan have worked? Maybe, but Wile E. should have been more careful. His freeze ray works too well! When the temperature is lowered enough, anything can be frozen into a solid—even wily coyotes!

freezing point—the temperature at which a liquid turns into a solid when cooled

Mighty Meltdown

Wile E. isn't ready to give up on freezing Road Runner just yet. He's got another idea to cool that bird off fast. With his ACME Instant Icicle Maker, Wile E. plans to make a tasty icicle treat out of Road Runner.

Look out Wile E.! Oops. Sometimes this coyote has the worst luck. But at least Wile E. won't be trapped in solid ice permanently. Luckily for him some solids, such as ice, easily melt back into liquids. He just needs to add some heat.

As the sun's powerful rays heat up the ice, the water molecules start moving faster. The more heat Wile E. adds, the faster the molecules move. Eventually the ice hits its **melting point** and turns into liquid water. Poor Wile E.! He's free from the ice, but it's going to take some time for him to warm up.

melting point—the temperature at which a solid turns into a liquid when heated

Operation Evaporation

Wile E. is trying an old trick to capture Road Runner. He's using a glass of water as bait. No thirsty bird can resist a cool glass of water in the desert. When Road Runner stops for the water, Wile E. plans to drop an ACME Mega-Cage to catch him. Wile E. thinks it's a foolproof plan. And it might be, if only he remembered how easily water changes its state.

FREE DRINK OF WATER

With enough heat, a liquid can change into a gas. This process is called **evaporation**. As the sun's energy heats the liquid water, its molecules move faster and faster. Eventually they gain enough energy to escape into the air as a gas called water vapor.

FREE DRINK OF WATER

Silly coyote! Simple evaporation ruined your sneaky plan. If you had placed the water in some shade, it wouldn't have evaporated as quickly. Better luck next time Wile E.!

evaporation—changing from a liquid into a gas

109

The Condensation Sensation

Wile E. has come up with a wet and wild idea this time. He just needs to add some rainwater to get Road Runner to slide right into his trap.

To make rain, Wile E. has to start with **condensation**. During this process, gases change into liquids as they cool down. Wile E.'s ACME Rainstorm Machine imitates nature to create rain. As it lowers the air temperature, water vapor molecules slow down. They collect around bits of dust in the air to create millions of tiny water droplets that form clouds. The droplets then begin joining together until they become too heavy and fall as raindrops.

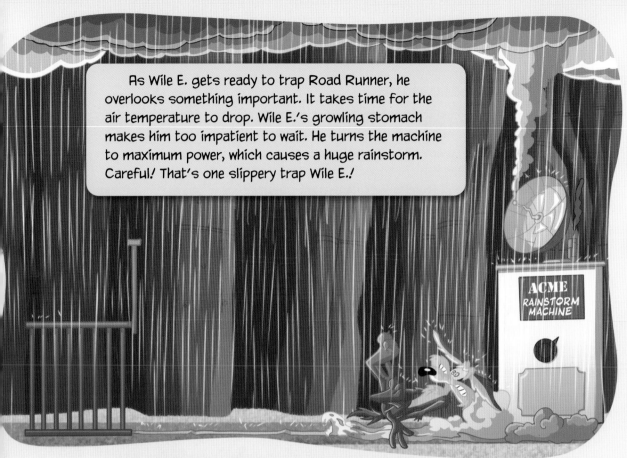

As Wile E. gets ready to trap Road Runner, he overlooks something important. It takes time for the air temperature to drop. Wile E.'s growling stomach makes him too impatient to wait. He turns the machine to maximum power, which causes a huge rainstorm. Careful! That's one slippery trap Wile E.!

ACME
RAINSTORM
MACHINE

condensation—changing from a gas to a liquid

A Sticky Situation

Wile E. thinks Road Runner won't resist a scoop of cold ice cream on a hot day. But will that silly coyote ever learn? Doesn't he remember that matter can physically change its state when heat is added? When Wile E.'s tasty ice cream melts, Road Runner just runs right past the ice cream puddle.

However, physical changes don't change the kind of molecules that make up matter. During a physical change, the chemical properties of matter stay the same. Although it's melted, the liquid ice cream is still made of the same sweet-tasting molecules.

FREE ICE CREAM

Physical changes are usually reversible—they can be undone. With one zap of the Freeze Ray, Road Runner can turn the liquid ice cream back into a solid again. And with Wile E. frozen solid, Road Runner can take his time eating all the ice cream he wants. Poor Wile E.! He didn't just miss out on a tasty meal. He also has a serious case of brain-freeze!

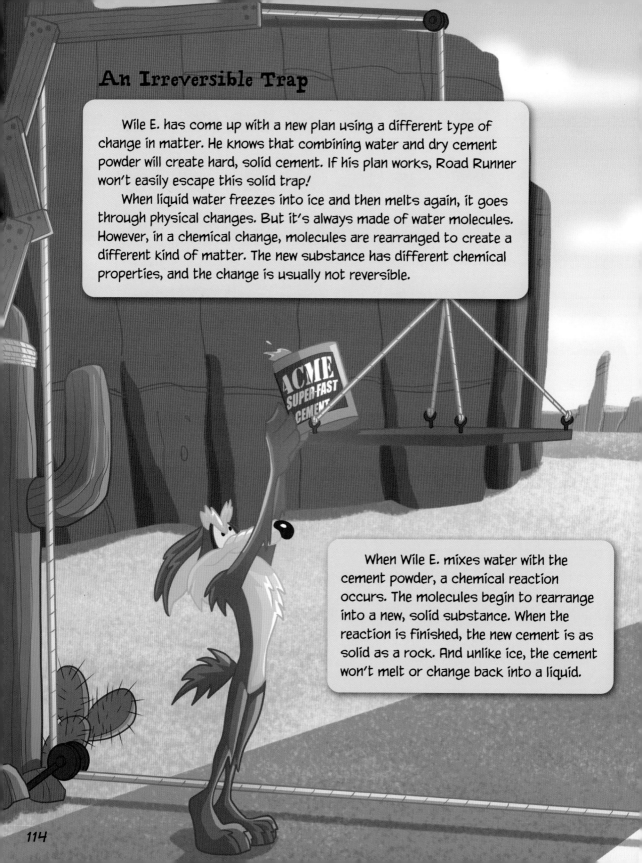

An Irreversible Trap

Wile E. has come up with a new plan using a different type of change in matter. He knows that combining water and dry cement powder will create hard, solid cement. If his plan works, Road Runner won't easily escape this solid trap!

When liquid water freezes into ice and then melts again, it goes through physical changes. But it's always made of water molecules. However, in a chemical change, molecules are rearranged to create a different kind of matter. The new substance has different chemical properties, and the change is usually not reversible.

When Wile E. mixes water with the cement powder, a chemical reaction occurs. The molecules begin to rearrange into a new, solid substance. When the reaction is finished, the new cement is as solid as a rock. And unlike ice, the cement won't melt or change back into a liquid.

Unfortunately for Wile E., he used ACME Super-Fast Cement mix. When his trap accidentally dumps the cement on him, it hardens in no time and traps him fast. You should have been more careful, Wile E.! Instead of catching Road Runner, you've become a popular spot for other desert birds.

115

Matter Matters

Wile E. has tried using different kinds of matter to capture Road Runner. He's experimented with solids, liquids, and gases. He's tried to freeze Road Runner, catch him in a rainstorm, and even trap him in cement. But nothing seems to work. However, Wile E. is one determined coyote. He isn't about to give up.

Wile E. has one more plan to try. He's created a beautiful ice sculpture to lure Road Runner into his trap. With a sparkling crown of dynamite, Wile E. is sure this trap will provide him with a tasty meal of roasted bird.

But it looks like Wile E. still hasn't learned much about how the states of matter work. Under the hot desert sun, his beautiful ice sculpture quickly melts. It doesn't take long for the liquid water to flow and carry the dynamite to where Wile E. is hiding.

Watch out, Wile E.! A powerful and irreversible chemical change is about to happen. Maybe next time Wile E. will remember how physical states and chemical changes in matter work. Perhaps then he'll have more success catching that speedy Road Runner.

THUD!

by
Mark Weakland

illustrated by
Christian Cornia

Wile E. Coyote
Experiments with
FORCES and MOTION

Flying with Force

Poor Wile E. Coyote. If only he could catch that tasty Road Runner. From rolling rocks to rocket sleds, his crazy schemes set all sorts of things into motion. But his plans never seem to work. If Wile E. just understood the science of forces and motion, he might nab that speedy bird.

STOP GO

Coyote
(Hungrius carnivorii)

mass—the amount of material in an object
accelerate—to increase the speed of a moving object

Whether sitting still or speeding down the road, Wile E. and Road Runner must both obey the laws of motion. These laws can be summed up as three general rules:

The Three Laws of Motion

1. An object at rest will stay at rest until a force moves it. Similarly, an object in motion will stay in motion unless an opposing force stops it.
2. An object's speed increases or decreases based on its **mass** and the forces acting on it.
3. Every force has an equal and opposite force.

OUCH !

The laws of motion direct how Wile E. moves and how quickly he **accelerates**. They also determine how hard he hits when he crashes into a telephone pole. Sometimes the laws of motion can hurt! Let's take a closer look at some of Wile E.'s crazy schemes and discover why his ideas go so wrong.

Road Runner
(Speedius birdius)

121

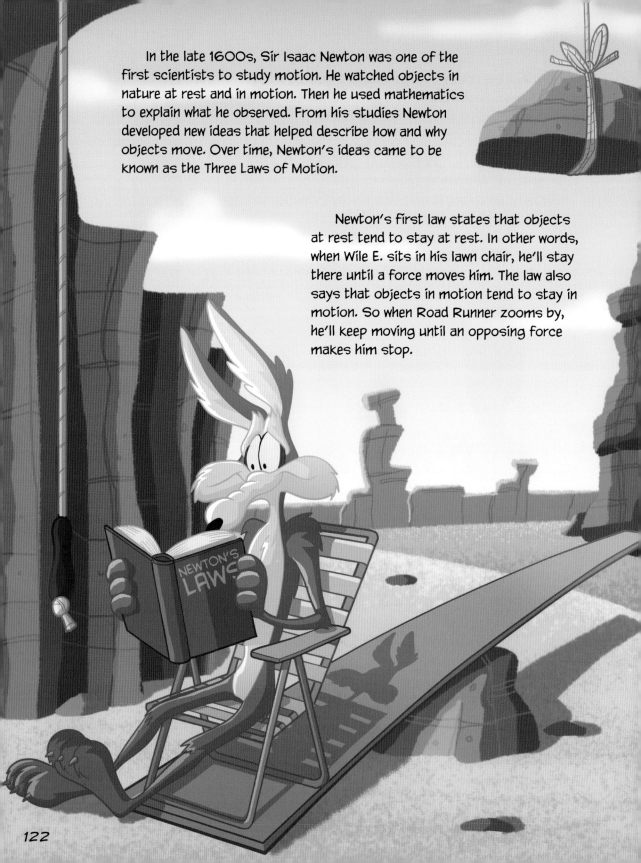

In the late 1600s, Sir Isaac Newton was one of the first scientists to study motion. He watched objects in nature at rest and in motion. Then he used mathematics to explain what he observed. From his studies Newton developed new ideas that helped describe how and why objects move. Over time, Newton's ideas came to be known as the Three Laws of Motion.

Newton's first law states that objects at rest tend to stay at rest. In other words, when Wile E. sits in his lawn chair, he'll stay there until a force moves him. The law also says that objects in motion tend to stay in motion. So when Road Runner zooms by, he'll keep moving until an opposing force makes him stop.

TWANG

Newton's second law says that an object's speed increases or decreases based on its mass and the forces acting on it. For example, Road Runner has a certain mass. While running, he needs to add a certain amount of force to his legs if he wants to run faster.

Finally, Newton's third law states that forces all have an equal and opposite force. If a giant boulder slams down on Wile E.'s seesaw, the other end will spring up with equal force. Wile E. should have thought about Newton's third law before dropping that boulder!

Chapter 1: Moving into Motion

Setting Objects in Motion

Road Runner is in a state of constant motion. To catch him, Wile E. needs to get himself moving too. In other words, he needs to exert a force. A force, which is a push or a pull, is what makes an object move. Newton's First Law of Motion tells us about **inertia**. This idea says that an object at rest, such as a coyote, will stay that way unless a force acts on him.

What kind force will set Wile E. into motion? Wile E. can force his legs to push against the ground. When his legs push down, the ground pushes back with equal force. The ground pushes against his feet to move him forward.

inertia—the tendency of an object to remain either at rest or in motion unless affected by an outside force

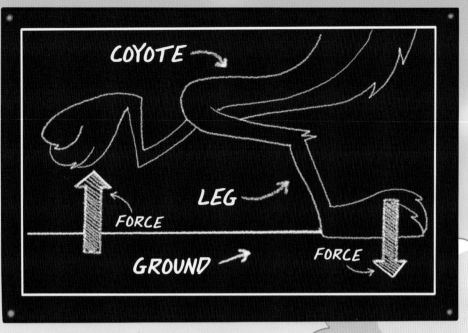

COYOTE

LEG

FORCE

GROUND

FORCE

Unfortunately for Wile E., his scrawny legs can't exert enough force to catch up to Road Runner.

Stopping an Object

Wile E. runs fast, but he'll need more than leg force to catch Road Runner. He can get a boost from Acme's Super Spring Sneakers. With every step, the force of his muscles combines with the force of the sneaker springs.

According to Newton's First Law of Motion, the inertia of Wile E.'s forward motion will continue until another force acts on him. In other words, he'll keep springing forward until something makes him stop.

BOING!

Road Runner can use the force of his legs to stop. But Wile E. has a problem. With all the Super Spring force behind him, he can't stop very easily.

WHACK!

Only a strong opposing force can stop Wile E.'s forward motion. Unfortunately for him, a rock wall provides the force needed. Ouch!

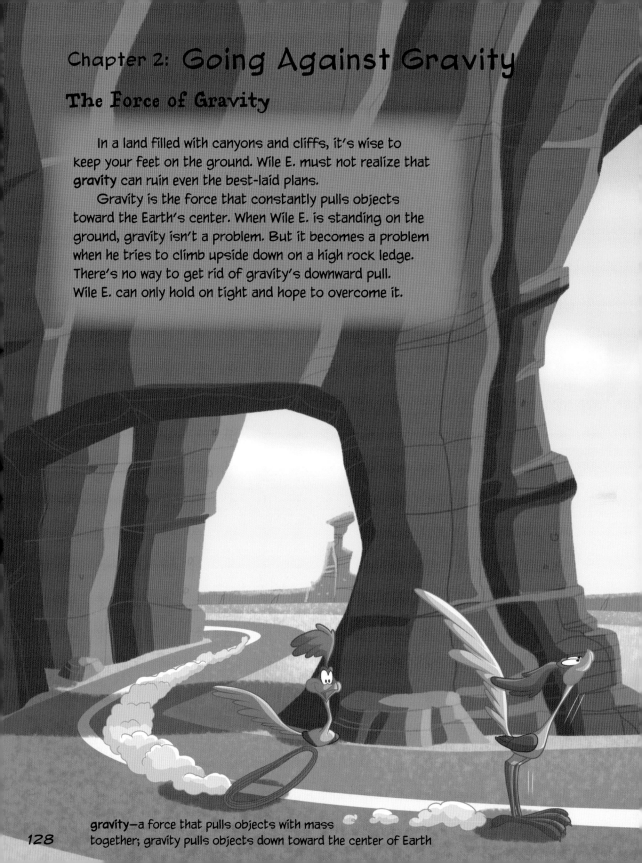

Chapter 2: Going Against Gravity

The Force of Gravity

In a land filled with canyons and cliffs, it's wise to keep your feet on the ground. Wile E. must not realize that **gravity** can ruin even the best-laid plans.

Gravity is the force that constantly pulls objects toward the Earth's center. When Wile E. is standing on the ground, gravity isn't a problem. But it becomes a problem when he tries to climb upside down on a high rock ledge. There's no way to get rid of gravity's downward pull. Wile E. can only hold on tight and hope to overcome it.

gravity—a force that pulls objects with mass together; gravity pulls objects down toward the center of Earth

gravity

Gravity's force is forever trying to pull resting bodies into motion. Wile E.'s grip may be strong, but it's not enough to overcome gravity's downward pull. Poor Wile E. never realized the gravity of his situation.

MEEP MEEP

FREE BIRD SEED

Counteracting Gravity

To counteract gravity's pull, Wile E. needs a strong opposing force. His hands aren't strong enough to provide the force he needs. But Wile E. Coyote, "Science Genius," always has a plan. He's going to try his new Acme Super Suction Cups.

gravity

Suction cups provide the force Wile E. needs to overcome gravity. They stick to a surface by using the force of air **pressure**. But Wile E. has forgotten an important fact. As gravity pulls on him, it also pulls on the rock ledge he's clinging to. When the rock cracks, gravity brings everything crashing down.

pressure—a force that pushes or pulls on something

But at least Wile E. won't fall forever. Soon the canyon floor will provide a force to stop his downward motion. Then Wile E. and the falling rock will come to rest.

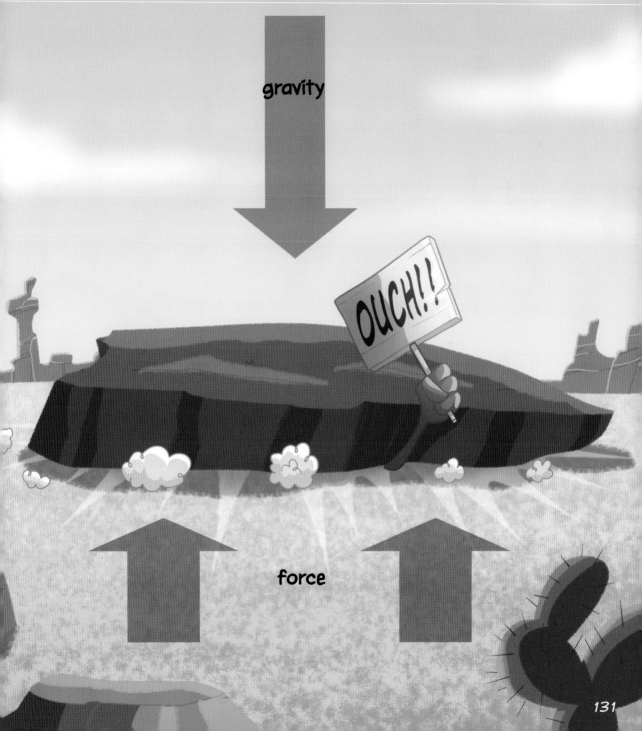

gravity

force

Lift and Air Resistance

It is possible to overcome gravity's pull and stay in the air for long periods of time. Wile E. knows that birds and airplanes beat gravity every day. And he thinks a coyote can too.

Wile E. tries using a pair of wings to get the lifting force he needs to defeat gravity. The wings' shape causes air to flow quickly over the top and more slowly along the bottom. The difference in airflow creates high pressure on the bottom of the wings and lower pressure above them. The high pressure pushes up on the wings to force them and Wile E. into the sky.

Of course, if the wings are damaged, they won't work correctly. No wings means no lift. And no lift means gravity will pull Wile E. to the ground. Sorry, Wile E.!

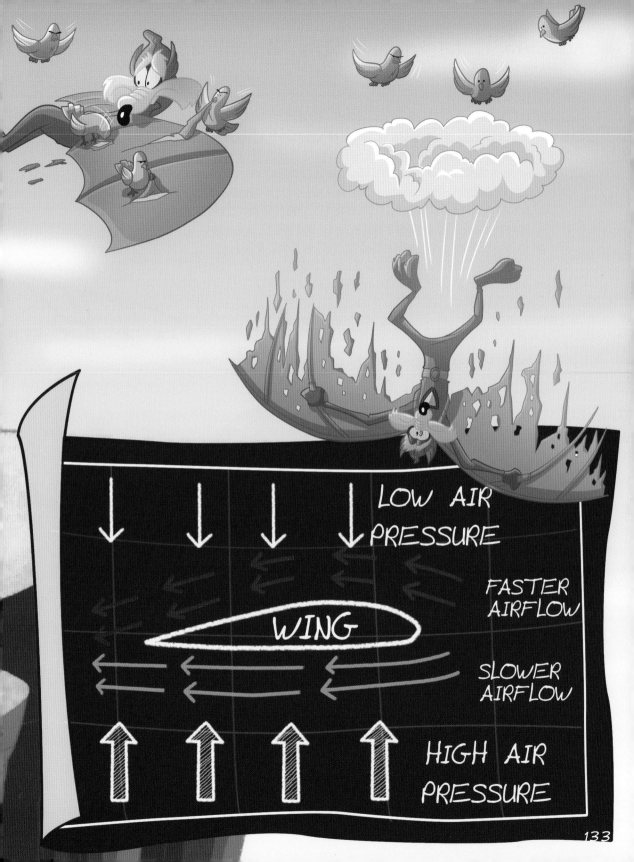

Chapter 3: Momentous Moments

Acceleration

Wile E. hasn't had much luck so far. To match Road Runner's speed, he needs to accelerate quickly. Wile E. thinks his new Acme Super Rocket Car will help him do just that!

Newton's Second Law of Motion can help Wile E. determine how much acceleration he needs. The law says that acceleration is the amount of force needed to move an object with a certain mass. In this case the objects are Wile E. and his rocket car. The amount of acceleration needed to catch Road Runner depends on the total mass of Wile E. and the car. Other forces acting on the car also affect its acceleration.

When the rocket engine applies a strong force to the car, it moves forward very quickly. As Wile E. increases the engine's power, more force is applied to the car's tires. This in turn causes the car to move forward faster and faster. In other words, it accelerates.

Acceleration is thrilling, but it can be risky. With too much of it, Wile E. could zoom past Road Runner and head straight into trouble. He also needs to remember Newton's First Law—objects in motion tend to stay in motion.

Moving with Momentum

Lots of acceleration leads to lots of speed. As Wile E. is about to learn, lots of speed can be dangerous. Like any moving object, a speeding rocket car has **momentum**. Momentum can be thought of as how difficult it is to stop a moving object. The more mass an object has, the more difficult it is to stop. Wile E.'s rocket car has a lot of mass. Combine that mass with high speed, and the rocket car has a lot of momentum.

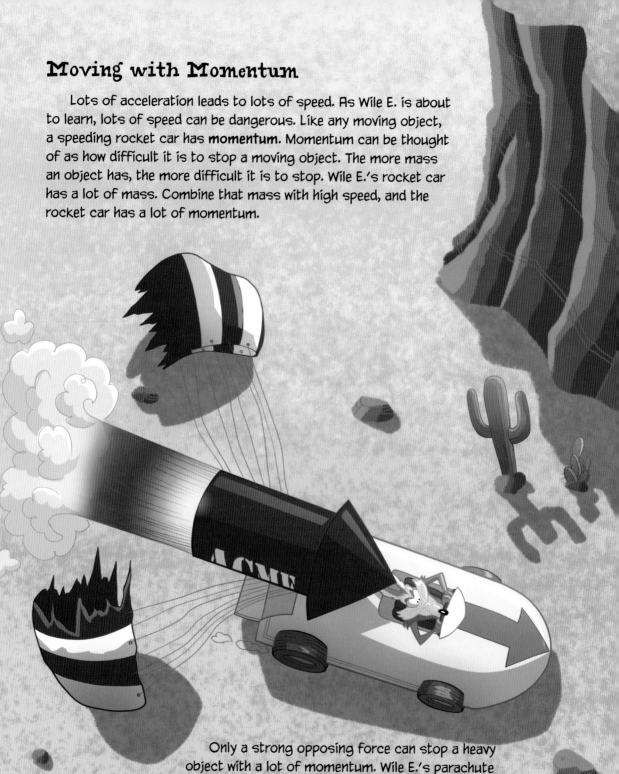

Only a strong opposing force can stop a heavy object with a lot of momentum. Wile E.'s parachute can't provide enough force to stop the car. Can sagebrush or cactuses provide the force he needs?

Sorry, Wile E. Only the canyon floor can provide a force strong enough to stop your speeding car.

CRASH

momentum—the amount of force in a moving object determined by the object's mass and speed

Changing Direction

Wile E. claims to be a genius, but he must have forgotten another part of Newton's First Law of Motion. The First Law says that a moving object keeps moving in the same direction until a force acts on it.

Road Runner can change direction by changing the angle of his legs and feet. As his legs push sideways against the road, they change the direction of his body. This sideways force works the same as the front wheels of a car. When a car's front tires are turned by the steering wheel, the sideways force changes the direction of the car.

But Wile E.'s Desert Surfer lacks something important—a steering wheel! He has no way to turn its front wheels and change its direction. The Desert Surfer will keep moving forward in a straight line until another force acts on it. Time to hit the brakes, Wile E.!

Friction

Uh-oh. Wile E.'s Desert Surfer is missing more than a steering wheel. It has no brakes! Fortunately, the force of **friction** seems to be slowing it down.

Friction is a force that counteracts motion. Friction slows objects down as they rub against one another. As the wheels of the Surfer rub against the ground, the force slows their rotation and the Surfer's speed. But the amount of friction between the wheels and the ground is small. The speed is reduced only a little.

friction—a force created when two objects rub together; friction slows down objects

However, Wile E. can create more friction by leaning back to drag the Surfer's back end on the ground. When there is a lot of friction, moving objects slow down quickly.

SKREEECH

But friction also produces heat. This is why your hands get warm when you rub them together quickly. Wile E. is really feeling the heat now!

Chapter 4:
Lights ... Camera ... Action ... Reaction!

Action and Reaction

Wile E. doesn't realize it, but he's about to experience Newton's third and most famous law of motion. The law states that for every force, there is an equal and opposite force.

Wile E. is getting ready to fire an Acme Mobile Cannon at Road Runner. But nobody told him about the gun's **recoil**. The recoil is the opposing force that matches the forward momentum of the cannonball. In a heavy gun like a cannon, the recoil force is transferred from the cannon's mount to the ground. But Wile E. forgot to lock the cannon's wheels. When he fires it, the cannon will roll backward as the cannonball flies forward.

recoil—the kickback of a gun when firing

Tricky Laws of Motion

Wile E. has worked hard on his latest scheme. Look closely and you'll see Newton's laws of motion at work. But Wile E. still hasn't learned much about them. When he sets the boulder into motion, its mass creates momentum that is difficult to stop. The boulder's action causes a reaction that Wile E. doesn't expect.

Figuring out forces and motion is tricky business. One mistake can ruin even the best plans. Will Wile E. ever be able to catch that speedy Road Runner? If he ever wants to succeed, he'll have to study the laws of forces and motion more closely in the future.

145

WHOOSH!

WILE E. COYOTE
EXPERIMENTS WITH
FLIGHT
AND
GRAVITY

by MARK WEAKLAND
illustrated by ALAN BROWN

It's a Bird!

It's a bird, it's a plane, it's ... a flying coyote! But not for long. Wile E. wants more than anything to catch Road Runner. But to do it, he needs to make better use of science.

Coyote
(Hungrius carnivorii)

Road Runner
(Speedius birdius)

Anything that flies must fight against **gravity**. Gravity is a force that is always working to bring things down. Birds beat gravity every day. So do mosquitoes. But people and coyotes can't fly. To overcome gravity, they have to use science.

Wile E. is learning this the hard way. To stay up longer and come down softer, he needs lessons on gravity and flight. Let's get him started.

gravity—a force that pulls objects with mass together;
gravity pulls objects down toward the center of Earth

Speed

A roller-blading coyote? You may see stranger things before this is all over. To get ready to fly, Wile E. must learn about **speed**. Speed is how fast an object moves at any given moment. As Wile E. moves across the desert, he travels at a constant speed. Right now his speed is 3 meters per second, or 3 m/s.

Wile E. can see that Road Runner is faster than he is. To increase his speed, Wile E. adds more force. The force comes from moving his legs. Unfortunately for Wile E., Road Runner can apply force too. Even a hard-working, roller-blading coyote can't catch that bird.

speed—rate of motion or progress

Velocity

To avoid a shocking situation, a flying coyote needs to know about **velocity** as well as speed. Velocity is the rate of change in an object's position. Think of it as speed with a direction. Let's say Wile E. is moving at 50 m/s, and he is flying east. Wile E.'s velocity is 50 m/s, east. When Road Runner changes direction and runs south, Wile E. changes direction too. Now Wile E.'s velocity is 50 m/s, south.

velocity—the speed an object travels in a certain direction

During a flight, the pilot always knows the plane's velocity. He or she also knows the velocity of the wind blowing on the plane. Knowing both helps the pilot plan for a smooth and safe flight.

Wile E. can change his velocity while flying. In other words, he can change his speed and direction. When Road Runner speeds up and heads west, Wile E. increases his speed and changes direction. But he forgot to fly higher off the ground. **ZAP!**

Velocity and Acceleration

Back on the ground, Wile E. is getting a lesson on **acceleration**. Wile E. uses the force of his legs to push himself across the flat desert. When he comes to a hill, he stops pushing. If Wile E. is no longer pushing, why does he keep moving? He moves because the force of gravity is pulling him. As gravity pulls, Wile E. gains speed. Soon he is rolling faster and faster down the hill. Wile E.'s direction is also changing. Now he is moving south instead of west.

acceleration—a change in velocity

A change in speed or direction is a change in velocity. A change in velocity is called acceleration. Acceleration can happen to anything that moves, such as a car, plane, or rolling coyote. Look out below!

CHAPTER 2

GRAVITY BRINGS YOU DOWN

Gravity Is a Force

Poor Wile E. doesn't know how strong Earth's gravity is. Every object in the universe has gravity. Tiny grains of sand have gravity. So do planets and stars. All objects on Earth experience gravity as a constant acceleration toward the center of the planet. It doesn't matter how heavy or light they are.

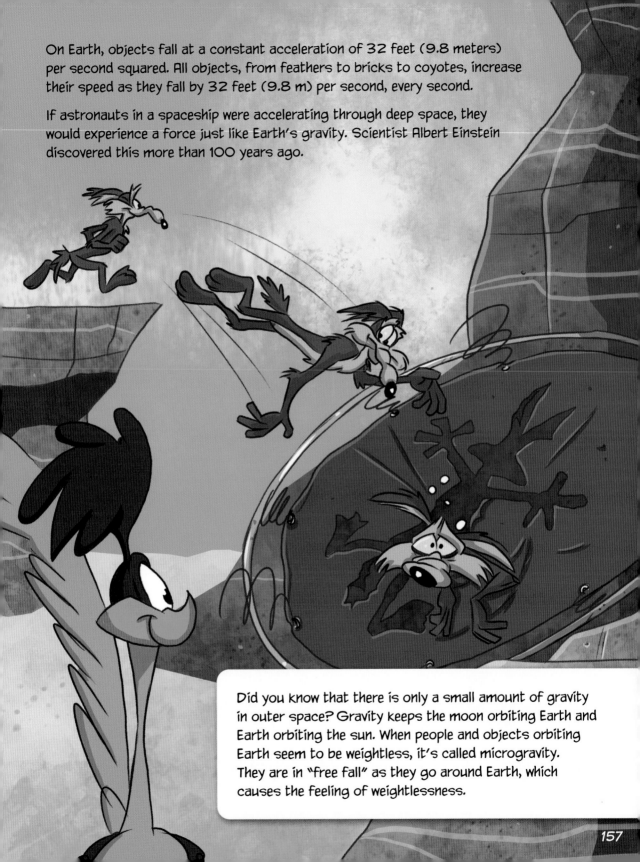

On Earth, objects fall at a constant acceleration of 32 feet (9.8 meters) per second squared. All objects, from feathers to bricks to coyotes, increase their speed as they fall by 32 feet (9.8 m) per second, every second.

If astronauts in a spaceship were accelerating through deep space, they would experience a force just like Earth's gravity. Scientist Albert Einstein discovered this more than 100 years ago.

Did you know that there is only a small amount of gravity in outer space? Gravity keeps the moon orbiting Earth and Earth orbiting the sun. When people and objects orbiting Earth seem to be weightless, it's called microgravity. They are in "free fall" as they go around Earth, which causes the feeling of weightlessness.

Gravity on Other Planets

Wile E. decides to try out gravity on the moon!
Other planets and moons have gravity too. But the
amount of gravity depends on mass. A planet or moon
with a small mass has a small amount of gravity.

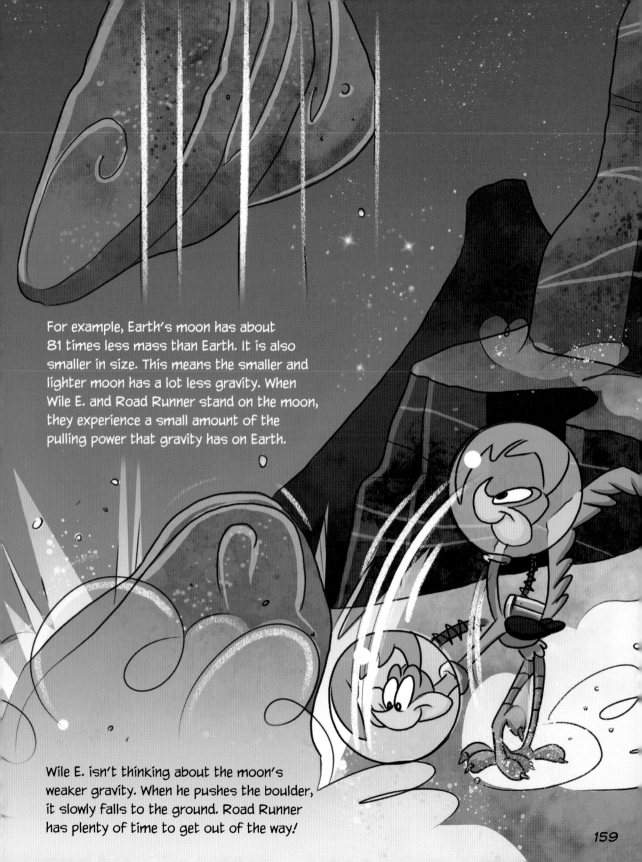

For example, Earth's moon has about 81 times less mass than Earth. It is also smaller in size. This means the smaller and lighter moon has a lot less gravity. When Wile E. and Road Runner stand on the moon, they experience a small amount of the pulling power that gravity has on Earth.

Wile E. isn't thinking about the moon's weaker gravity. When he pushes the boulder, it slowly falls to the ground. Road Runner has plenty of time to get out of the way!

CHAPTER 3

UP, UP, AND AWAY

Counteracting Gravity

Wile E. thinks Earth's gravity is easier to deal with. Back on Earth when Wile E. leaps, gravity takes over and pulls him down. Wile E. needs a strong force to work against gravity. He has chosen air **resistance**.

Air resistance, or drag, is a force that slows an object's fall. To see drag in action, drop a paper clip and a sheet of paper. Because gravity gives constant acceleration no matter the object's mass, both the paper clip and paper should hit the ground at the same time. The paper clip doesn't have a lot of drag, so it falls at a typical rate. But the sheet of paper has more surface area. This creates a lot of drag. Drag slows the paper's fall.

Just like the sheet of paper, Wile E.'s parachute creates drag. This slows his fall. When a strong gust of wind blows into his parachute, another force acts on it. This force is called **lift**. Lift works against gravity. Wile E. rises, and his plan is ruined.

lift—the upward force that causes an object to rise in the air

resistance—a force that opposes or slows the motion of an object; friction is a form of resistance

Air Speed and Lift

Wile E. knows that birds and airplanes beat gravity every day. And he thinks a coyote can too. A pair of wings should give Wile E. the lift he needs to beat gravity and get off the ground.

Wings work by moving the air around them. Wile E.'s plane wings push more and more air away as they pick up speed. Even more air moves when Wile E. moves the wings in a specific direction.

Lift presses up on an airplane's wings as air is increasingly moved away. All this upward pressure forces the wings and Wile E. into the sky. Wile E. is flying!

Of course if the wings are damaged, they won't work correctly. No wings mean no lift. And no lift means that gravity pulls the plane and Wile E. to the ground.

pressure—exertion of force upon a surface; force per unit area

Lift and Weight

Gravity constantly acts on Wile E.'s plane. But other forces act on it as well. Lift is one force. When Wile E. sits on the ground, he has no lift. But he does have weight, which is caused by his mass in the presence of gravity. To move his weight and the weight of his plane off the ground, Wile E. drives his plane forward. As the wings push away the air, they create lift.

lift

gravity

As Wile E.'s plane goes faster and faster, more and more air is pushed away. Air pressure increases under the wings. Soon lift will exceed gravity. When this happens, the plane rises. As long as Wile E. keeps a high enough air speed, the plane will stay in the air.

So why does Wile E. crash? As he slows down to net Road Runner, his plane loses lift. Soon there is not enough lift to overcome gravity.

Drag and Thrust

You can't keep a good coyote down. This time Wile E. won't slow his plane's speed. He'll also use a bigger engine, which will make more **thrust**.

Thrust and drag are two more forces that act on Wile E.'s plane. A plane's engine creates thrust. Thrust moves the plane forward down the runway and through the air. Drag works against thrust. It comes from the air resistance that pulls on the plane as it moves through the air. If the plane's engine thrust is greater than the air's drag, the plane accelerates forward. But if the drag becomes too great, the plane slows down.

drag

thrust

thrust—the force that pushes a vehicle forward

Pilots pull in a plane's wheels when flying. They do this for the same reason birds tuck in their legs. Legs and wheels create drag, which slows them down. When Wile E. gets ready to use his capture box, the box creates a lot of drag. This slows the plane down and allows Road Runner to get away. What a drag!

Equilibrium

Wile E. has learned that lift, gravity, thrust, and drag are the forces acting on his plane. All four forces must be balanced for a steady flight. When all the forces are balanced, they are in **equilibrium**.

When they are not in equilibrium, any number of things can happen. If the thrust is greater than the drag, the plane accelerates forward. If the drag is greater than the thrust, the plane slows down. If lift is greater than gravity, the plane accelerates upward. And if gravity is greater than lift, the plane accelerates downward.

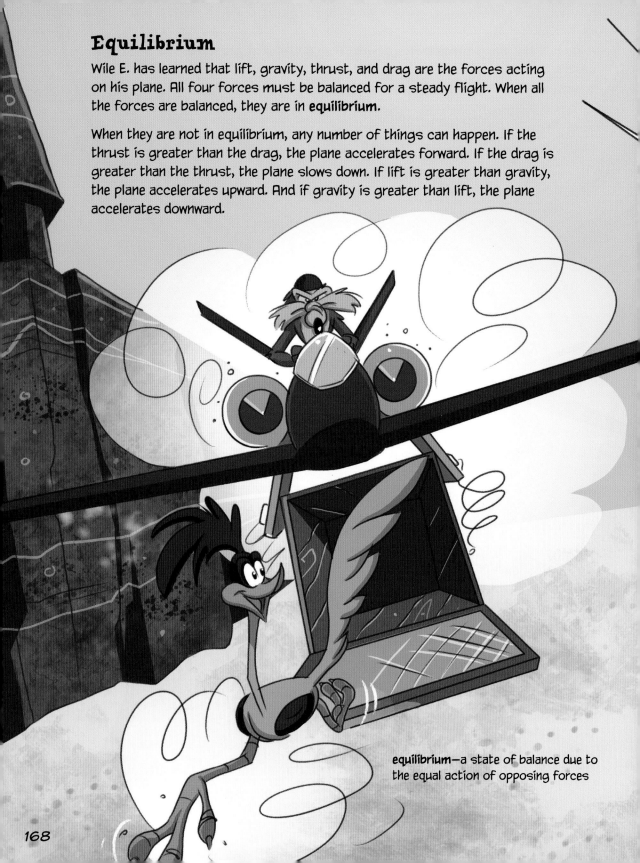

equilibrium—a state of balance due to the equal action of opposing forces

Now Wile E. can relax. Even with the capture box, he is having a steady flight. Of course, there is more to flying than just forces. Wile E. needs to watch where he's going!

Orbital Velocity

It's Wile E. Coyote, rocket scientist! He's learned that some flying machines don't have to deal with four forces.

Only three forces act on a rocket during takeoff. A rocket flies straight up and does not need wings to provide lift. So a rocket only deals with thrust, gravity, and drag. Gravity and drag hold the rocket down. Thrust moves it upward.

To get into orbit, a spacecraft must move upward very quickly. This is called **orbital velocity**. On Earth, the orbital velocity is around 7,800 m/s. That's 17,600 miles per hour!

Once in space, only gravity and thrust act on a spaceship. Lift and drag do not factor into a ship's flight because there is no air in space. Hopefully Wile E. will jump off before he gets that high!

orbital velocity—the speed an object needs to reach in order to orbit Earth

Wile E. looks a bit down, don't you think? Even though things aren't looking up for him, Wile E. has learned a lot. He knows acceleration is a change in velocity. He knows gravity is a force. He understands that all objects experience gravity. He sees that gravity and drag bring things down. And he knows that lift and thrust help birds and planes fly. It looks like Wile E. could use a little lift right now!

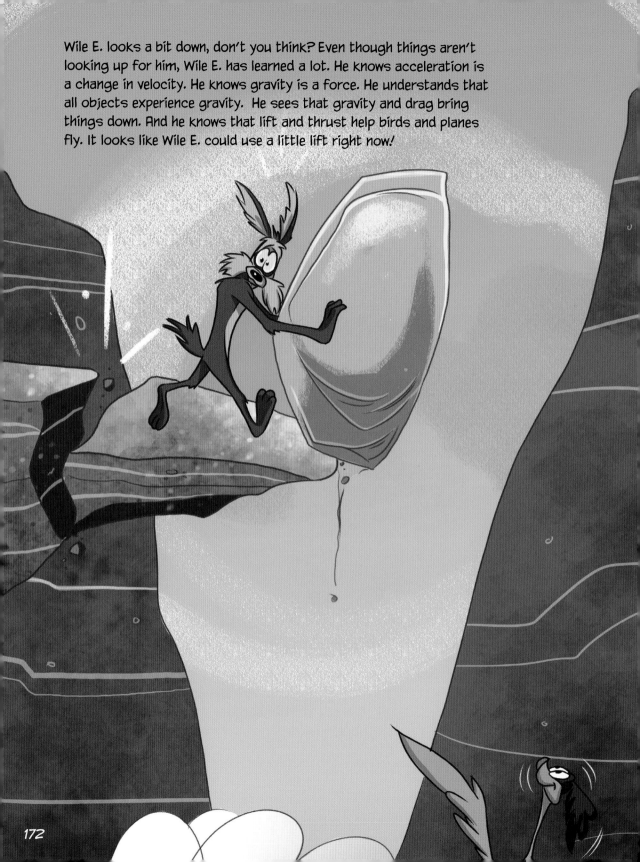

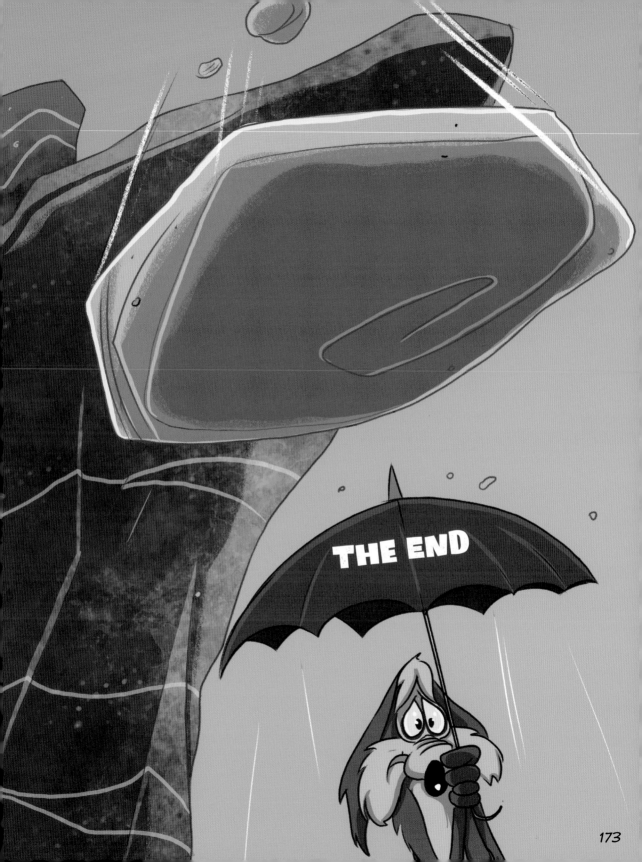

Wile E. Coyote
Experiments with
ENERGY

by Suzanne Slade

illustrated by
Andrés Martínez Ricci

ZAP!

Introduction:
Powered Up with Energy

   Wile E. Coyote always has one thing on his mind—capturing that speedy, delicious Road Runner! Wile E. keeps trying out new inventions that use energy. But if he's ever going to succeed, he needs to understand how energy works.

Road Runner
(Speedius birdius)

Coyote
(Hungrius carnivorii)

Energy is the ability for something to do work, such as moving or lifting things. There are many kinds of energy, including electrical, chemical, mechanical, heat, light, and more. Wile E. knows that he needs a lot of energy to catch Road Runner. He just needs to learn which kind will work best and how to use it correctly!

Changing Energy

If Wile E. did his homework, he'd see that energy is all around him. He'd also see that energy often changes from one type into another.

Wile E.'s newest plan uses energy stored in **fuel** to help him soar after Road Runner. The engines in his ACME Flyer burn fuel. As it burns, the fuel's energy is changed into different types that can be used to do work. Some of the energy is turned into sound and heat. But the rest becomes mechanical energy that turns the Flyer's propellers and helps Wile E. fly through the air.

Wile E. thinks he's pretty smart. But he's forgotten something important. Fuel produces only a limited amount of energy. Once it's used up, it has to be replaced. Just as Wile E.'s stomach can't run on empty, his engines can't run without fuel. Too bad he forgot to bring some extra gas before he jumped off the cliff!

fuel—anything that can be burned to give off energy

Chapter 1: Energy in Motion

Spring into Potential

He doesn't realize it yet, but Wile E.'s next plan could cause him some trouble. He thinks his new ACME Super Spring will give him the boost he needs to grab Road Runner. His plan could work. But he needs to know more about how his spring works.

When Wile E. squeezes or stretches the spring, it gains and stores up **potential energy**. The more the spring is squeezed or stretched, the more potential energy it has.

potential energy—the stored energy of an object that is raised, stretched, or squeezed

Wile E. plans to use the spring's stored up energy to launch himself toward Road Runner. He wants to get moving fast, so he squeezes the spring as tight as possible. As Wile E. waits for Road Runner, the energy stored in the spring waits too. When he releases the spring, its stored energy changes into mechanical energy. The spring shoots out and quickly pushes Wile E. after Road Runner.

Unfortunately, Wile E. overlooked the second part of how springs work. As the spring pushes him forward, it stretches out and gains potential energy again. When the spring can't stretch any more, that energy again turns into mechanical energy. The spring quickly returns to its normal size and pulls Wile E. into the rock. Ouch!

On the Move

What's Wile E. up to now? He's fixing up a seedy snack with an extra surprise. Road Runner is always on the move, so Wile E. plans to get moving too. With his ACME Super Magnet and some iron birdseed, he's on the go in no time.

Kinetic energy is the energy of motion. Any type of motion—up, down, sideways, backward, or forward—is considered kinetic energy. The amount of kinetic energy an object has depends on its **mass** and speed. Mass is the amount of **matter** in an object. An object's kinetic energy increases if its mass or speed increases.

As Wile E. rolls faster and faster after Road Runner, his kinetic energy keeps increasing. Unfortunately for Wile E., other objects can have kinetic energy too. He's about to learn that a big train has tons of mass. This means that it has tons of its own kinetic energy too. Look out, Wile E.! That train isn't going to stop!

kinetic energy—the energy of things in motion
mass—the amount of material in an object
matter—anything that has weight and takes up space

Chapter 2: Electrical and Chemical Energy

It's Electric!

If Wile E. is going to catch the speedy Road Runner, he needs something with a lot more energy. He's sure that his new electric ACME Trap-O-Matic will bring success. Too bad there's nowhere to plug it in. Instead, Wile E. thinks he can hook his machine directly to the power lines running overhead. But that probably isn't the best idea.

To understand electricity, Wile E. needs to know about tiny particles called atoms. All matter is made up of atoms. Each atom has a **nucleus** made of protons and neutrons. Protons carry a positive electrical charge, while neutrons have no charge. Atoms also have negatively charged electrons that circle around the nucleus. Electrons can break free from atoms and flow between atoms in wires and other **conductors**. As the electrons flow, they create an electrical **current**. This electrical power can be used in many ways. When used properly, electricity is a safe and helpful source of energy.

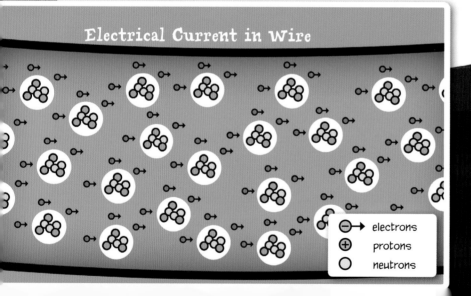

Electrical Current in Wire

⊖→ electrons
⊕ protons
○ neutrons

But Wile E. doesn't seem to realize how easily electricity flows through metal objects like wire. It can be very dangerous. Don't touch that wire, Wile E.! Oops, too late. Hopefully Wile E. learned a lesson. He should always keep his distance from electrical power lines.

Action! Reaction!

Wile E.'s first electrical scheme didn't work out. But this "Super Genius" thinks he knows how chemical and electrical energy work and is ready for action. When he fires up his battery-powered Super Scooter, the chase is on!

The battery in Wile E.'s scooter uses two different chemicals to create electrical energy. The chemical in the negative end of the battery carries extra electrons. The positive end has another chemical with too few electrons. The middle of the battery contains a barrier that keeps the two sides separate. When Wile E. connects his scooter's motor to the battery, electrons begin flowing to create an electrical current. The electrical power flows through the wires and the motor to make the scooter go.

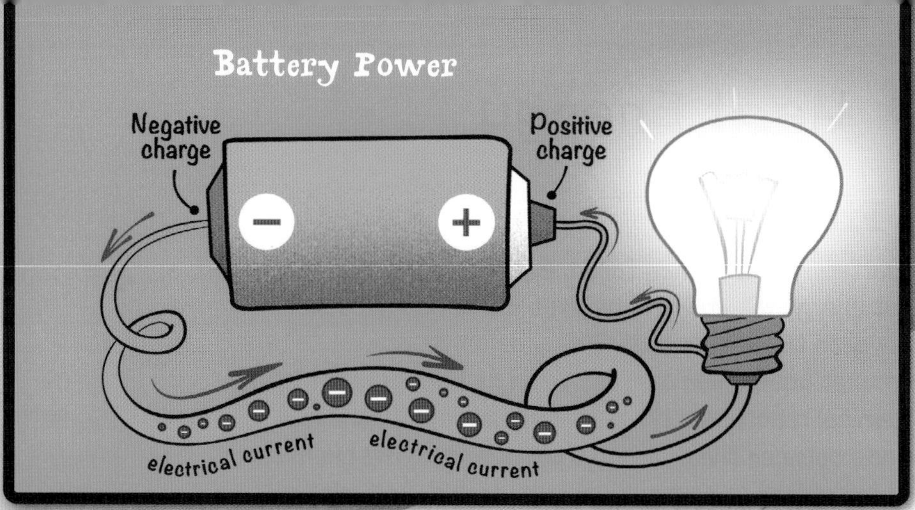

Battery Power

Negative charge

Positive charge

electrical current   electrical current

Uh-oh! The battery in Wile E.'s scooter is dead. Too bad he didn't know that batteries don't last forever. Maybe next time he'll remember to use a fully-charged battery before chasing Road Runner.

OH NO!

Chapter 3: Heat Energy

Fuel the Fire

Wile E.'s battery-powered plan failed. But he's sure that his new plan using heat energy will work. He believes his powerful rocket will help him finally grab that tasty bird.

Wile E.'s rocket uses chemical fuel. When he lights the fuse, it starts a chemical reaction in the fuel's **molecules.** As the fuel burns, the bonds between the molecules break apart. The chemical energy stored in the fuel is changed to light, sound, and a lot of heat energy. The hot gases from the burning fuel are then forced out the back of the rocket. The process of burning the fuel changes its chemical energy into kinetic energy as the rocket blasts off.

Wile E. was right about one thing. The rocket fuel definitely provides a lot of energy. But it's a lot more than he was ready for. Wile E. should have remembered to use his seat belt!

molecule—two or more atoms bonded together to make the smallest unit of a substance

Hidden Heat

Wile E. has tried a lot of crazy ideas, but his plans never seem to work. Now he's thinking that a simpler plan might work better. This time he's going to use the heat under his feet to make some Road Runner soup. He just needs Road Runner to fall for his clever hot tub trick.

Deep inside Earth, temperatures reach up to 180,000 degrees Fahrenheit (100,000 degrees Celsius). These high temperatures create hot spots inside Earth's crust. These spots often create pockets of hot water and steam. Scientists drill into these pockets to capture Earth's natural **geothermal** energy. The hot water and steam is then used to spin **turbine generators** to create electricity. Geothermal energy can also be used to heat buildings. Some people even use natural hot springs for bathing.

Wile E.'s found the perfect place to cook up his dinner. It's just the right temperature for making delicious Road Runner soup. But he forgot one important thing—super-heated ground water also creates **geysers!**

Relaxing
Hot Tub
FREE
for Road Runners

Relaxing
Hot Tub
FREE
for Road Runners

CHOOOM!

geothermal—relating to the intense heat inside Earth
turbine generator—a machine that produces electricity as a fluid passes through curved blades attached to it
geyser—an underground spring that shoots hot water or steam through a hole in the ground

191

Chapter 4: Renewable Energy Sources

Fun in the Sun

It's another hot day in the desert, and Wile E. is cooking up a new idea to get a mouthwatering dinner. He's hoping the sun will give his solar-powered car plenty of energy to catch up to Road Runner.

The fuel used in rockets or engines is nonrenewable. It can only be used once. But **renewable energy** sources like solar power are always available. Wile E.'s car is covered with solar panels. Each panel contains dozens of solar cells. When sunlight shines on the cells, a small amount of electricity flows between the layers inside. Thin metal strips in the cells capture this electricity and conduct it to larger wires. The electricity then flows to the car's motor. The motor then turns it into mechanical energy to power the car.

MEEP MEEP

Wile E. is off! He knows the sun won't run out of energy
quickly like batteries or rocket fuel. But it looks like Wile E.
is in the dark about how solar energy works. He needs to stay
in the sunlight to keep his engine running!

renewable energy—power from sources that will
not be used up, such as wind, water, and the Sun

The Wild, Wild Wind

Wile E. is ready to set sail in his latest contraption—the ACME Land Sailer. When the wind's energy pushes his sailer at high speed, Wile E. is sure that he can catch Road Runner this time.

As the sun beats down, it heats up the air above the desert. When the warm air rises, cooler air moves in to take its place. This air movement creates wind, which has a lot of energy that can be captured and used. Power companies use huge wind turbine generators to capture the wind's energy. The wind spins the turbine blades that are attached to the generator. The generator then changes the wind's energy into electrical energy to power homes and businesses.

SHWOOSH!!!

Wile E. knows that wind power is a renewable source of energy. But he must not realize that it isn't reliable or predictable. It can stop blowing, change direction, or be blocked. Without warning, the wind can start blowing again. Too bad for Wile E., the wind can also blow so hard it sends him sailing right over a cliff!

Wonderful Water Power

Ahoy, matey! Captain Coyote is riding the rapids to catch up with Road Runner. Wile E. knows the river has plenty of kinetic energy to get him moving. But he didn't know about that huge dam in front of him. Good thing he dove off his jet ski just in time!

But Wile E. isn't safe yet. He can't escape the water's strong current, which pulls him into the dam. This dam is part of a **hydroelectric** power plant. Water rushes through a long tube near the base called a penstock. The powerful flow of water pushes Wile E. around and around with the blades of a turbine generator. The generator turns the water's kinetic energy into electricity, which is sent to nearby homes. Like wind and solar power, hydroelectric power is another type of clean, renewable energy.

Luckily Wile E. is good at holding his breath! Don't worry Wile E. Maybe you'll have more luck catching Road Runner next time.

hydroelectric—having to do with making electricity from the force of moving water

Energy from Waste

In the desert, the nearest gas station can be hundreds of miles away. Wile E. learned earlier that energy in regular fuel can run out fast. But this time he's going to try using a biomass car instead. Biomass is a natural and renewable energy source made from animal and plant waste. Some cars run on bioethanol, which is a liquid fuel made from corn.

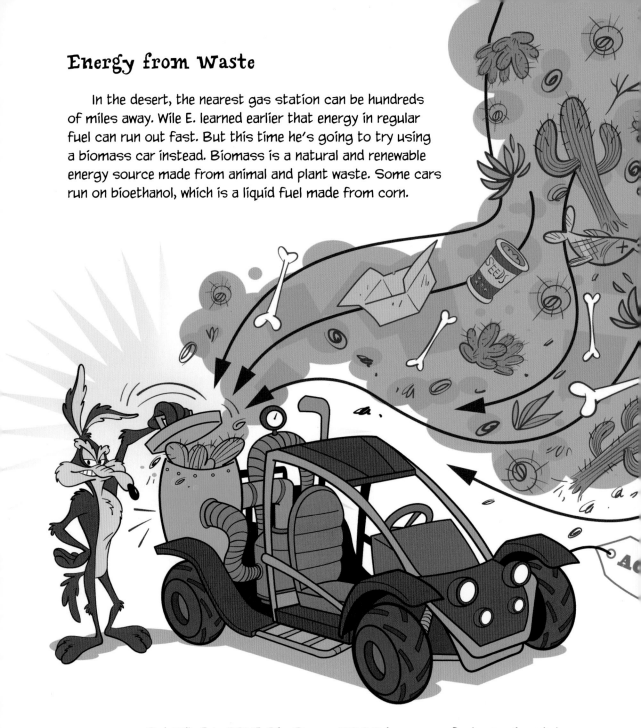

But Wile E.'s ACME Bio-Buggy 2000 is a super-fast experimental car. It can run on almost anything. As the car burns the biomass, the fuel's energy is turned into heat. That heat is then turned into mechanical energy to power the car. Fortunately for Wile E., there's plenty of biomass fuel available. He can use as much as he can find to power his new car.

Whoa, hold on Wile E.! You used too much fuel. This car and coyote are out of control!

CRASH!!!!

Energy is Everywhere

Wile E. is one hungry coyote. So he keeps trying to use different kinds of energy to capture Road Runner. He has tried using mechanical energy, electrical energy, and chemical energy stored in fuel. He's tried renewable energy from the sun, wind, and water. He even tried using heat energy from deep inside Earth. But he still hasn't caught that pesky Road Runner. Could the ACME Solar Hover-Car finally be the answer?

Maybe not. Wile E. can't count on clear skies. However, he can always count on one thing—energy is found everywhere. Energy gives Wile E. the ability to do work and move things, and to keep chasing Road Runner.

WHY ME?

BLAM!!

Unfortunately, Wile E. still has a lot to learn about how energy works. It seems to be hazardous to his health!

WILE E. COYOTE
EXPERIMENTS WITH
SPEED AND VELOCITY

ACME CO.

ZOOM!

by MARK WEAKLAND
illustrated by PACO SORDO

The Need for Speed

Look at Wile E. run! If he moved a bit faster, he could catch Road Runner. Oh! Road Runner changed direction. That bird can turn on a dime.

Road Runner
(Speedius birdius)

Racing and chasing are all about speed and velocity. Wile E. needs speed to beat Road Runner in a race. To follow Road Runner as he swerves, Wile E. needs to match Road Runner's velocity. If Wile E. knew more about speed and velocity, he could catch his quick-footed enemy.

Coyote
(Hungrius carnivorii)

Let's watch Wile E. go through his motions.
Maybe he'll learn a thing or two.

Speed Does Not Equal Velocity

Talk about running in circles! Wile E. is moving fast, but he's not really going anywhere.

Speed and velocity are part of the study of **motion**. Motion means a change in position. All motion is relative to a fixed point. Right now Wile E. and Road Runner are moving very fast, changing their positions very quickly. They move along a fixed path, past stationary signs.

Some might say both of them have great speed and velocity. People use the words "speed" and "velocity" as if they mean the same thing. They are related, but there is a difference between the two. Speed is how fast something is going. Velocity is speed plus a direction of motion.

motion—the action or process of moving or changing position

Speed

To catch Road Runner, Wile E. needs to know how fast the bird is going. He uses a radar gun to measure Road Runner's speed.

Speed is a measurement of how fast an object moves. The measurement is made up of two things—**distance** and time.

Distance is how far something travels. If a bird like Road Runner has a speed of 80 miles (129 kilometers) per hour, it can move a distance of 80 miles (129 km) in one hour.

speed = 0 mph

One more thing must be considered to measure speed—the reference point. For speed the reference point is usually the ground. If Wile E. walks at a speed of 3 mph (4.8 km/h), he is being compared to a road sign or another point that is at rest on the ground. Before Road Runner started running, he was standing still. His speed was zero. But after a few seconds, his speed was 80 mph (129 km/h).

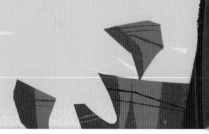

One of the first scientists to measure speed as distance over time was Galileo. More than 350 years ago, Galileo let balls roll down a ramp. As they rolled, he observed their motion. Galileo measured how far each ball moved within a certain amount of time. Today people use tools such as radar guns and anemometers to measure speed.

speed = 80 mph

speed = distance/time

distance—the length traveled between two points

Measuring Speed

Wile E. has some serious speed. But he still can't catch the bird. How many miles per hour does Wile E. need to go?

In the United States, speed on the highway is measured in miles per hour, or mph. But scientists measure speed in meters per second, or m/s. The speed of many things, including sound waves, spacecraft, and even light are measured in m/s. Speed through the air and across water is different though. Air and water speed are typically measured in knots. One knot is equal to traveling 1 nautical mile (1.15 miles) in one hour.

100 mph

The fastest possible speed in the universe is the speed of light in a vacuum, like outer space. Light speed is 299,792,458 meters per second. That's fast! The speed of light can also be written as 186,282 miles per second. That's right, not miles per hour, but miles per second! If you could travel at the speed of light, you could fly to the moon in less than one and a half seconds! Nothing can travel faster than light, not even Road Runner.

When light enters objects such as water or glass, it bends and slows down. This process is called refraction.

Average and Instantaneous Speed

Wile E. has a plan to travel faster. But he is making a mistake. He doesn't understand there are two kinds of speed.

Average speed describes the distance an object travels in a given amount of time. Let's say Road Runner ran for one hour. In that time he covered 400 miles (644 km). This means his average speed was 400 mph (644 km/h). During that hour he may have increased or decreased his speed. Maybe he slowed down to 395 mph (636 km/h) for a few seconds. Maybe he sped up to 410 mph (660 km/h) for a few seconds. At the end of the hour, he traveled a total of 400 miles (644 km). So his average speed was 400 mph (644 km/h).

Instantaneous speed is different. It is the speed of an object at a given moment. Right now Road Runner is traveling at 415 mph (668 km/h). But in the next moment, he may slow down to 405 mph (652 km/h). After that he may speed up to 417 mph (671 km/h). At each moment, he has a different instantaneous speed.

Wile E. goofed when he confused average speed with instantaneous speed. He also goofed when he thought sitting on a rocket was a good idea!

average speed—the distance an object has traveled divided by the time it has taken to travel that distance

instantaneous speed—the speed of an object at a given moment in time

Common Uses for Speed Measurement

It's useful to know an object's speed. Wile E. understands this. If he knows how fast a rock is traveling, he may be able to duck in time. Or he may not!

Knowing an object's speed comes in handy in everyday life. Pilots use their knowledge of speed to help them safely fly their planes. People measure wind speed to help predict weather. Truck drivers use their average speed to figure out when they will arrive at their final destinations. Police officers calculate a car's instantaneous speed to find out if the driver is breaking the speed limit.

CHAPTER 2

VIVA VELOCITY!

What Is Velocity?

Wile E. now knows about speed. But does he know anything about velocity? Let's find out.

Velocity is speed with direction. To find Road Runner's velocity, Wile E. must know Road Runner's speed and direction. Like speed, velocity is measured in meters per second. But velocity's measurement also gives an object's direction. For example, Wile E. is traveling at a velocity of 75 m/s, west. Road Runner is traveling at a velocity of 75 m/s, east. They have the same speed but different velocities.

Wile E. has the right speed for catching Road Runner. But he isn't traveling in the right direction. In the end Wile E. has only one direction to go. Down!

Average and Instantaneous Velocity

While trying to make a tar pit trap, Wile E. got his drill bit stuck. Now the drill's motor is spinning him at a speed of 13 m/s. This means that he travels a distance of 13 meters every second.

Wile E.'s head is really spinning. He knows velocity has to do with a change in position. And boy, is he changing position! But because he is moving in a circle, Wile E. keeps coming back to the same spot. So his average velocity is zero. However Wile E.'s instantaneous velocity is definitely not zero, since he is moving.

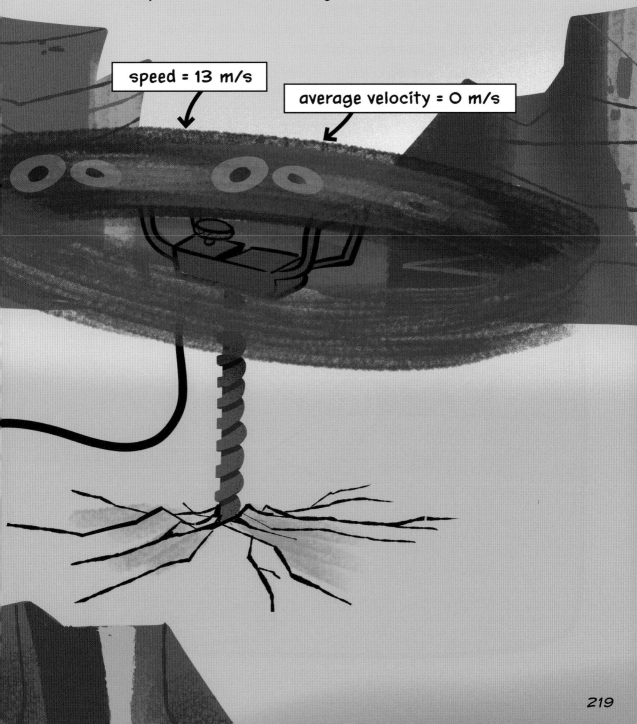

speed = 13 m/s

average velocity = 0 m/s

Acceleration

Wile E. hasn't had much luck catching Road Runner. The bird can go from 0 to 60 mph (97 km/h) in three seconds flat! To catch his speedy enemy, Wile E. needs to accelerate quickly. He thinks his new ACME Super Rocket will help him do just that.

During **acceleration**, a moving object's velocity changes. Acceleration often describes how much speed an object is picking up. Newton's Second Law of Motion says a force, like a push, causes an object to accelerate. The larger the force, the more the object's acceleration will increase.

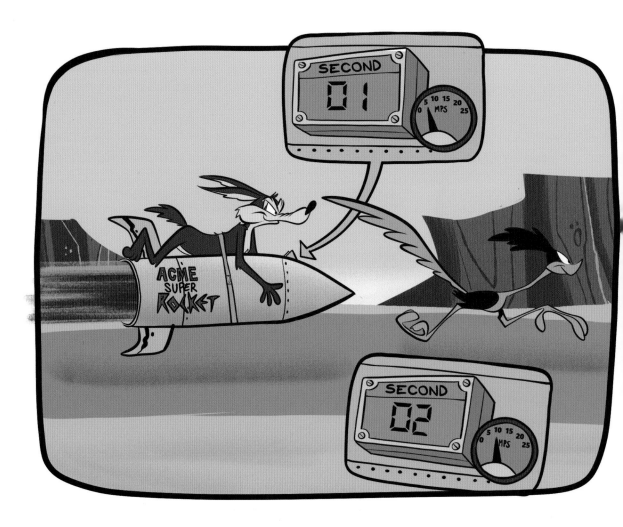

Acceleration can be measured every second. Take Wile E. on his rocket, for example. In the first second, his rocket is moving at a speed of 5 m/s. In the next second, its speed is 10 m/s. And in the third second, the rocket is moving at 15 m/s. The rocket's speed increased every second. This means it was accelerating. Because Wile E. was sitting on the rocket, he was accelerating too.

Will Wile E. keep accelerating? And if he does, where will he end up?

acceleration—the rate of change of the velocity of a moving object

Deceleration

As Wile E.'s rocket runs out of fuel, it **decelerates**. In other words, it slows down. Poor Wile E.!

Here comes Wile E. on his rocket. At first he is moving at 25 m/s. A second later he is moving at 20 m/s. And a second after that, his speed is 15 m/s.

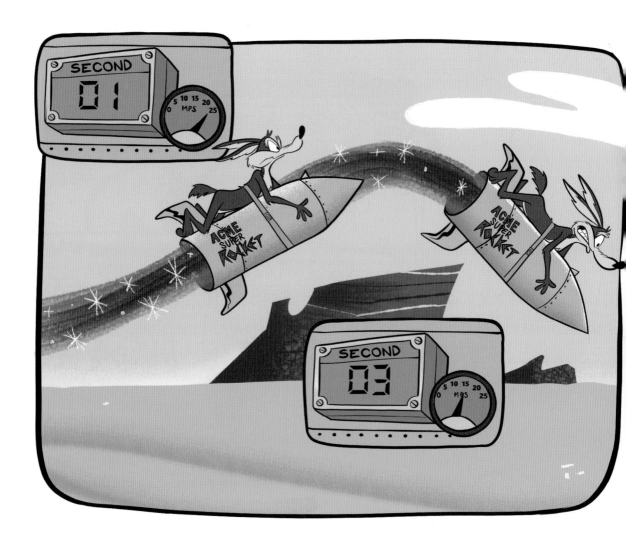

deceleration—a decrease in the velocity of a moving object

At every second of Wile E.'s motion, his speed was different. This looks a lot like acceleration. The difference is his speed is decreasing, not increasing. Wile E. is slowing down due to the force of **friction**. Until he falls off a cliff, that is!

friction—a force produced when two objects rub against each other; friction slows down objects

Wile E. is confused. Should he be thinking about distance or position?

A change in position is known as **displacement**. Displacement tells how far something moves in a specific direction. To get from point A to point B, Road Runner runs along a winding road. He travels 20 miles (32 km).

displacement—the shortest distance between two points

But a straight line shows his true change in position. The line starts at point A and ends at point B. If Road Runner runs this straight line, he only travels 9 miles (14 km). Nine miles (14 km) is his displacement, or his overall change in position. The average velocity is the displacement divided by the time it takes to get from point A to point B.

Common Uses for Velocity Measurement

An object's velocity is a very useful thing to know. Soldiers calculate velocity to make sure shells fired from big guns hit their targets. Wile E. could learn a thing or two from them!

Pilots use velocity to land airplanes. Rocket scientists calculate velocity all the time. They need to know a space probe's velocity before it can orbit Jupiter or Mars.

Passing a football has to do with velocity too. A quarterback judges how fast to throw the ball and in what direction to throw it. Think about when you play dodgeball at school. Every time someone throws a ball at you, you unconsciously calculate the speed and direction that the ball is moving so you don't get hit!

Speed and Velocity Matter

Can a speedboat help Wile E. catch Road Runner? Not if he's traveling in the wrong direction.

Even though Wile E. was often heading the wrong way, he still learned a lot. He learned that speed and velocity are two different things. Speed is about distance and time. Velocity is about distance, time, and direction.

It can be useful to know your speed and velocity. Drivers check their highway speed. If they are going too fast, they'll get a ticket. Pilots check their air velocity. If they come in from the wrong direction, they can't land safely.

Wile E. should be checking his speed and velocity too. It's the only way he'll ever catch Road Runner!

Key Physical Science Terms

acceleration (ak-sel-uh-RAY-shuhn)—the rate of change of the velocity of a moving object

atom (AT-uhm)—an element in its smallest form

attract (uh-TRAKT)—to pull something toward something else

average speed (AV-uh-rij SPEED)—the distance an object has traveled divided by the time it has taken to travel that distance

catalyst (CAT-uh-list)—a substance that speeds up a chemical reaction without being used up by the chemical reaction

charge (CHARJ)—the amount of electricity moving through something

chemical reaction (KE-muh-kuhl ree-AK-shuhn)—a process in which one or more substances are made into a new substance or substances

combustion (kuhm-BUS-chuhn)—burning; a fast chemical change that occurs when oxygen combines with another substance

compound (KAHM-paund)—a substance made of two or more elements bonded together

condensation (kahn-duhn-SAY-shuhn)—changing from a gas to a liquid

conductor (kuhn-DUHK-tuhr)—a material that lets electricity travel easily through it

current (KUHR-uhnt)—the flow of electrons

cylinder (SIH-luhn-duhr)—a shape with flat, circular ends and sides shaped like a tube

deceleration (dee-sell-uh-RAY-shuhn)—a decrease in the velocity of a moving object

density (DEN-sih-tee)—the amount of mass an object or substance has based on a unit of volume

distance (DIS-tuhns)—the length traveled between two points

electromagnet (ih-lek-troh-MAG-nuht)—a device consisting of an iron or steel core that is magnetized by electric current in a coil that surrounds it

electron (ih-LEK-tron)—one of the tiny particles that make up all things

element (EL-uh-muhnt)—a basic substance that is made up of only one kind of atom

enzyme (EN-zime)—a special protein that speeds up chemical reactions in the body

equilibrium (ee-kwuh-LIB-ree-uhm)—a state of balance due to the equal action of opposing forces

evaporation (ih-vap-uh-RAY-shun)—changing from a liquid into a gas

fluid (FLOO-id)—a liquid or gas substance that flows

freezing point (FREEZ-ing POYNT)—the temperature at which a liquid turns into a solid when cooled

friction (FRIK-shuhn)—a force created when two objects rub together; friction slows down objects

fuel (FYOOL)—anything that can be burned to give off energy fulcrum (FUL-kruhm)—a resting point on which a lever pivots

gravity (GRAV-uh-tee)—force that pulls objects with mass together; gravity pulls objects down toward the center of Earth

inertia (in-UR-shuh)—the tendency of an object to remain either at rest or in motion unless affected by an outside force

kinetic energy (kih-NET-ik EN-ur-jee)—the energy of things in motion

lift (LIFT)—the upward force that causes an object to rise in the air

load (LOHD)—an object that moves when a force is applied

magnetic field (mag-NET-ik FEELD)—a region of space near a magnet or electric current in which a magnetic force can act on another substance

mass (MASS)—the amount of material in an object

matter (MAT-ur)—anything that has weight and takes up space

melting point (MELT-ing POYNT)—the temperature at which a solid turns into a liquid when heated

molecule (MOL-uh-kyool)—two or more atoms bonded together to make the smallest unit of a substance

momentum (moh-MEN-tuhm)—the amount of force in a moving object determined by the object's mass and speed

motion (MOH-shuhn)—the action or process of moving or changing position

nucleus (NOO-klee-uhss)—the center of an atom

oxidizer (OK-suh-dize-ur)—a chemical that a fuel requires to burn

polarity (poh-LAYR-uh-tee)—having two oppositely charged poles

pole (POHL)—either of the two regions or parts of a magnet that exhibits magnetic polarity

potential energy (puh-TEN-shuhl EN-ur-jee)—the stored energy of an object that is raised, stretched, or squeezed

pressure (PRESH-ur)—the amount of force over a certain area

reaction rate (ree-AK-shuhn RAYT)—how fast or slow a reaction takes place

reagent (ree-AY-juhnt)—a substance that takes part in and undergoes change during a reaction

repel (rih-PEL)—to exert a force on an object so that the object is pushed away

resistance (rih-ZISS-tuhnss)—a force that opposes or slows the motion of an object; friction is a form of resistance

rotational motion (roh-TAY-shun-uhl MO-shun)—the motion of an object rotating around a fixed point

rotor (ROH-tur)—a rotating part of a machine

speed (SPEED)—rate of motion or progress

supersonic (soo-pur-SON-ik)—faster than the speed of sound

thrust (THRUHST)—the force that pushes a vehicle forward

velocity (vuh-LOSS-uh-tee)—the speed an object travels in a certain direction

Index